Siobhán

drawing
ROSINSKI
DUFAUX
script

Colour Work: GRAZA

9th CINEBOOK
The 9th Art Publisher

Original title: Complainte des landes perdues Cycle 1 – 1 Sioban

Original edition: © Dargaud Benelux (Dargaud-Lombard SA), 1993
by Dufaux & Rosinski
www.dargaud.com
All rights reserved

English translation: © 2013 Cinebook Ltd

Translator: Jerome Saincantin
Lettering and text layout: Patrice Leppert
Printed in Spain by Just Colour Graphic

This edition first published in Great Britain in 2013 by
Cinebook Ltd
56 Beech Avenue
Canterbury, Kent
CT4 7TA
www.cinebook.com

A CIP catalogue record for this book
is available from the British Library

ISBN 978-1-84918-169-3

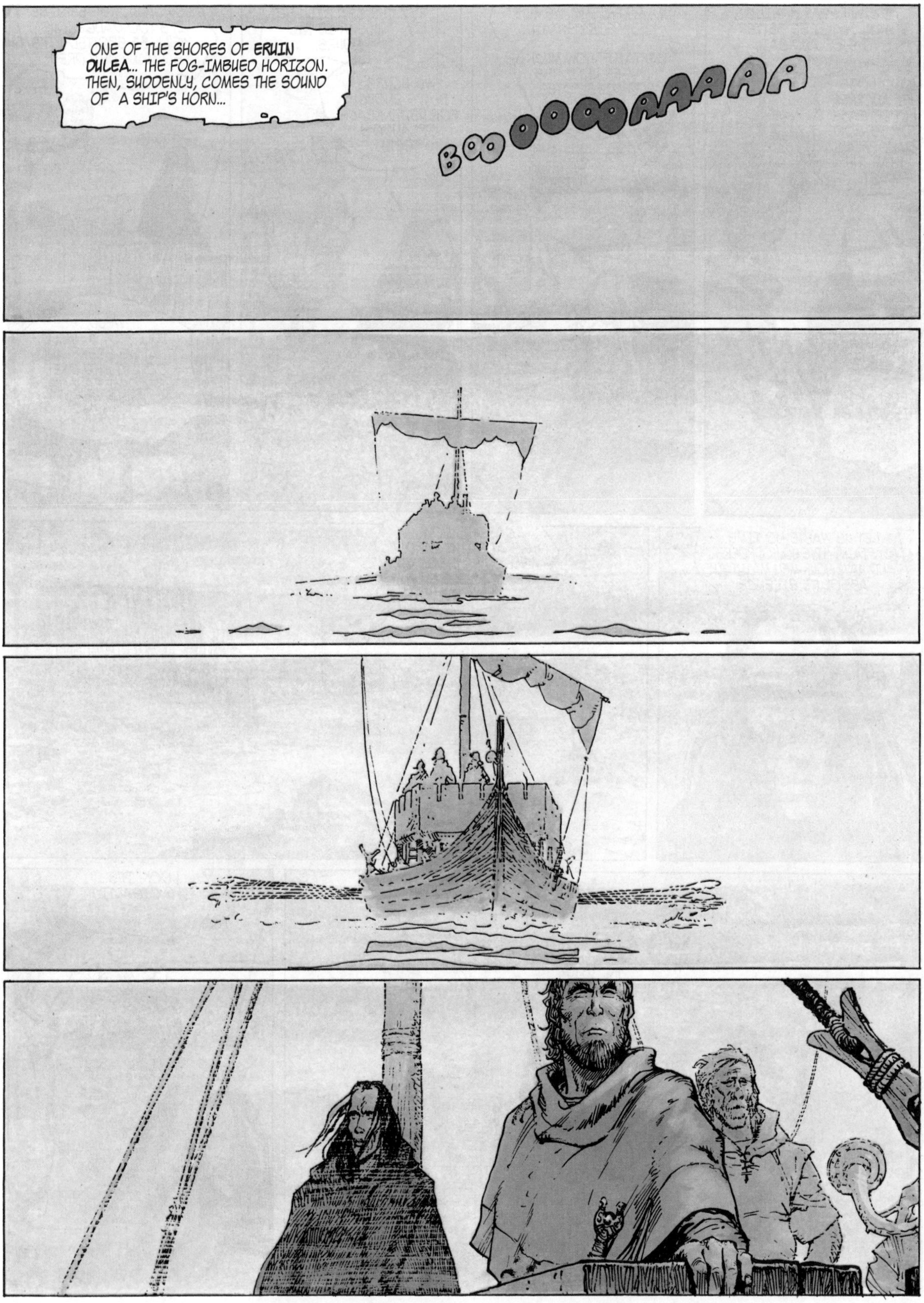
ONE OF THE SHORES OF **ERUIN DULEA**... THE FOG-IMBUED HORIZON. THEN, SUDDENLY, COMES THE SOUND OF A SHIP'S HORN...
BOOOOOOAAAAAA

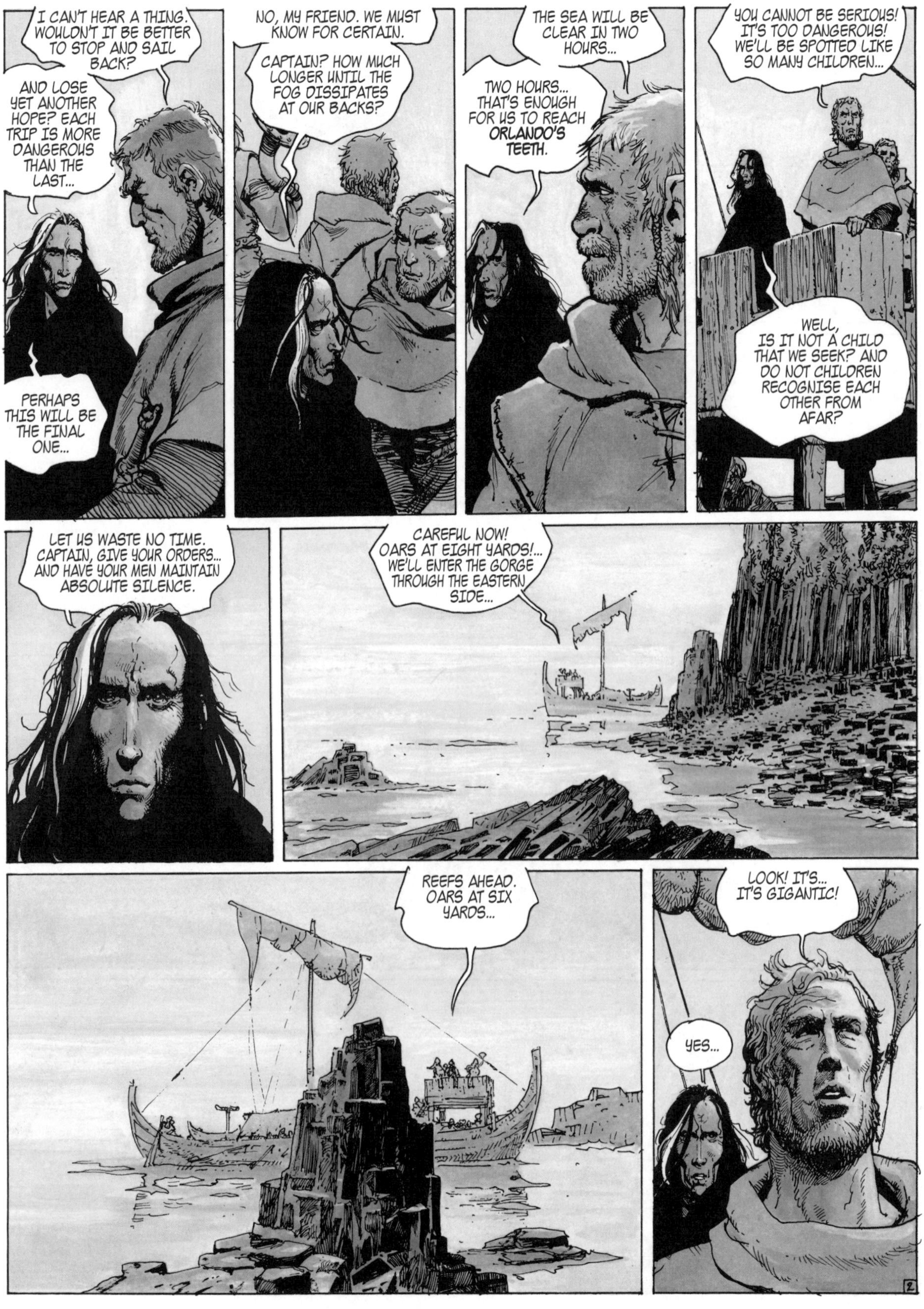
I CAN'T HEAR A THING. WOULDN'T IT BE BETTER TO STOP AND SAIL BACK?
AND LOSE YET ANOTHER HOPE? EACH TRIP IS MORE DANGEROUS THAN THE LAST...
PERHAPS THIS WILL BE THE FINAL ONE...
NO, MY FRIEND. WE MUST KNOW FOR CERTAIN.
CAPTAIN? HOW MUCH LONGER UNTIL THE FOG DISSIPATES AT OUR BACKS?
THE SEA WILL BE CLEAR IN TWO HOURS...
TWO HOURS... THAT'S ENOUGH FOR US TO REACH ORLANDO'S TEETH.
YOU CANNOT BE SERIOUS! IT'S TOO DANGEROUS! WE'LL BE SPOTTED LIKE SO MANY CHILDREN...
WELL, IS IT NOT A CHILD THAT WE SEEK? AND DO NOT CHILDREN RECOGNISE EACH OTHER FROM AFAR?
LET US WASTE NO TIME. CAPTAIN, GIVE YOUR ORDERS... AND HAVE YOUR MEN MAINTAIN ABSOLUTE SILENCE.
CAREFUL NOW! OARS AT EIGHT YARDS!... WE'LL ENTER THE GORGE THROUGH THE EASTERN SIDE...
REEFS AHEAD. OARS AT SIX YARDS...
LOOK! IT'S... IT'S GIGANTIC!
YES...
2

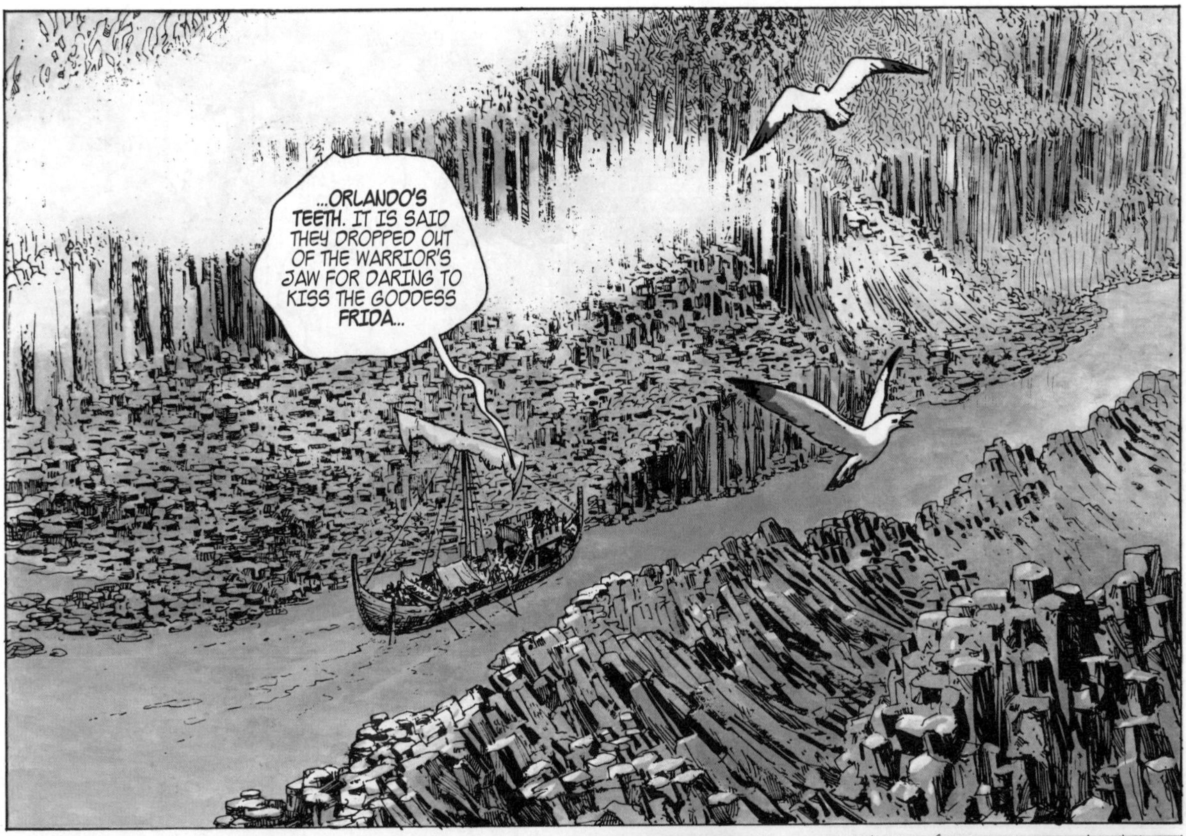
...ORLANDO'S TEETH. IT IS SAID THEY DROPPED OUT OF THE WARRIOR'S JAW FOR DARING TO KISS THE GODDESS FRIDA...

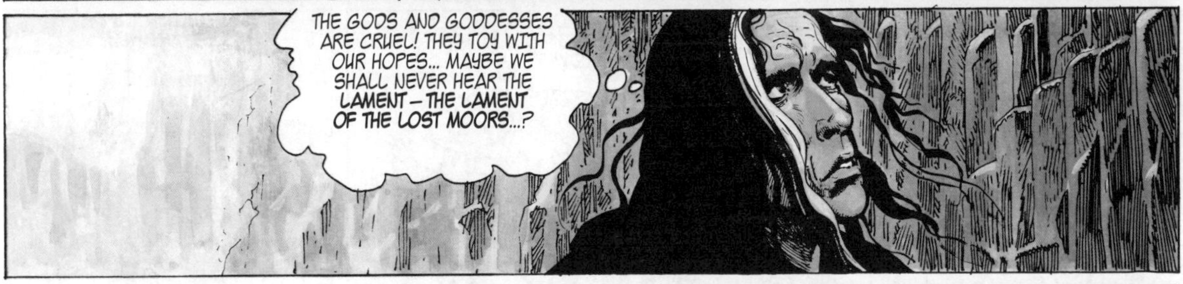
THE GODS AND GODDESSES ARE CRUEL! THEY TOY WITH OUR HOPES... MAYBE WE SHALL NEVER HEAR THE LAMENT – THE LAMENT OF THE LOST MOORS...?

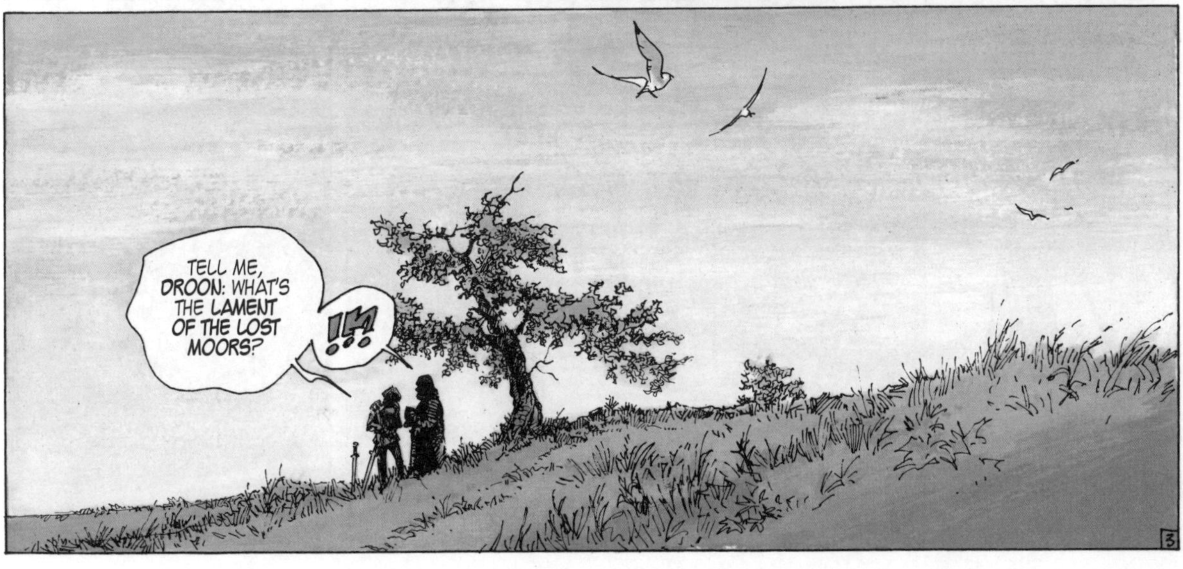
TELL ME, DROON: WHAT'S THE LAMENT OF THE LOST MOORS?
!!?!
3

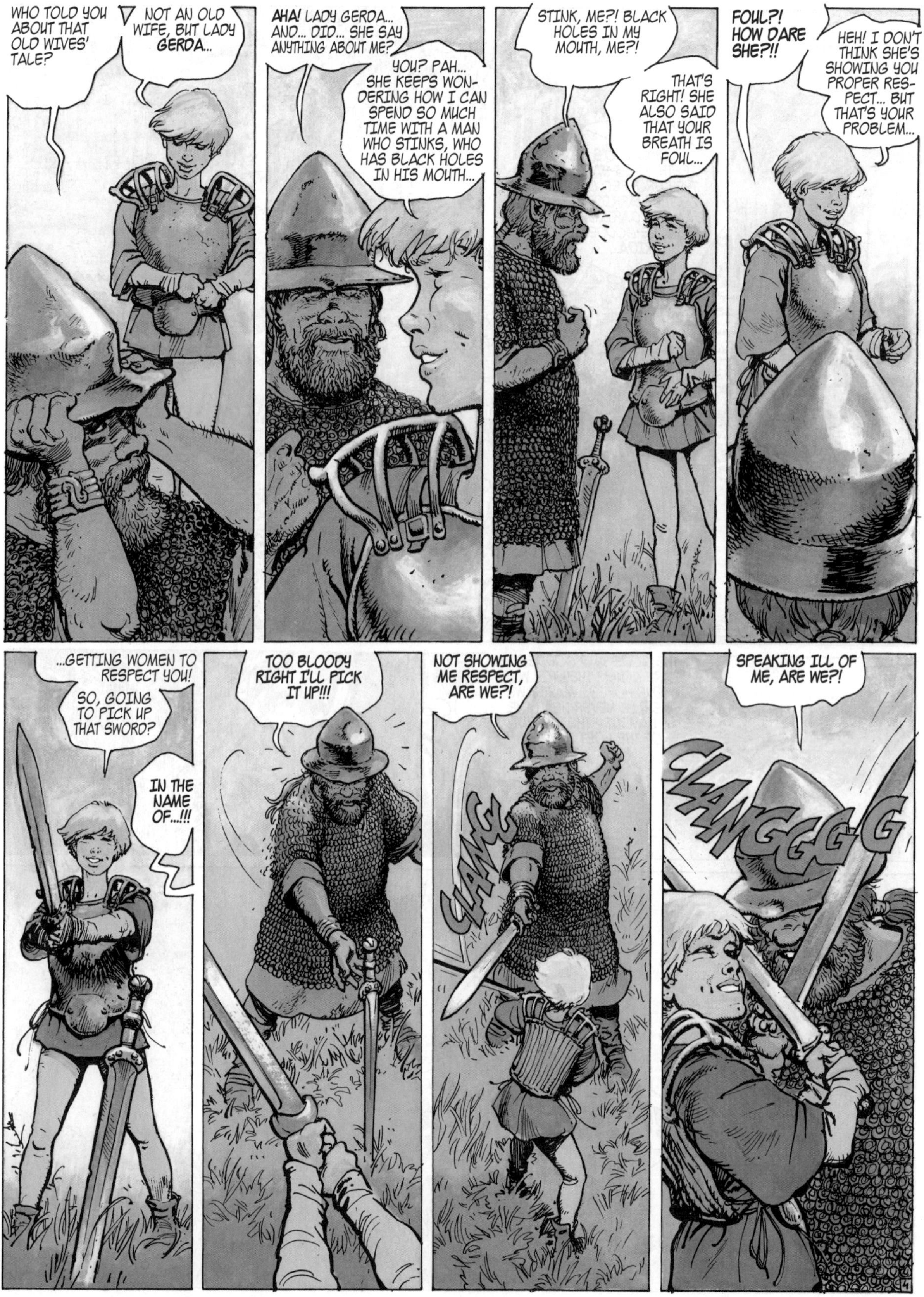

WHO TOLD YOU ABOUT THAT OLD WIVES' TALE?
NOT AN OLD WIFE, BUT LADY GERDA...
AHA! LADY GERDA... AND... DID... SHE SAY ANYTHING ABOUT ME?
YOU? PAH... SHE KEEPS WONDERING HOW I CAN SPEND SO MUCH TIME WITH A MAN WHO STINKS, WHO HAS BLACK HOLES IN HIS MOUTH...
STINK, ME?! BLACK HOLES IN MY MOUTH, ME?!
THAT'S RIGHT! SHE ALSO SAID THAT YOUR BREATH IS FOUL...
FOUL?! HOW DARE SHE?!!
HEH! I DON'T THINK SHE'S SHOWING YOU PROPER RESPECT... BUT THAT'S YOUR PROBLEM...
...GETTING WOMEN TO RESPECT YOU!
SO, GOING TO PICK UP THAT SWORD?
IN THE NAME OF...!!!
TOO BLOODY RIGHT I'LL PICK IT UP!!!
NOT SHOWING ME RESPECT, ARE WE?!
CLANG
SPEAKING ILL OF ME, ARE WE?!
CLANGGGGG

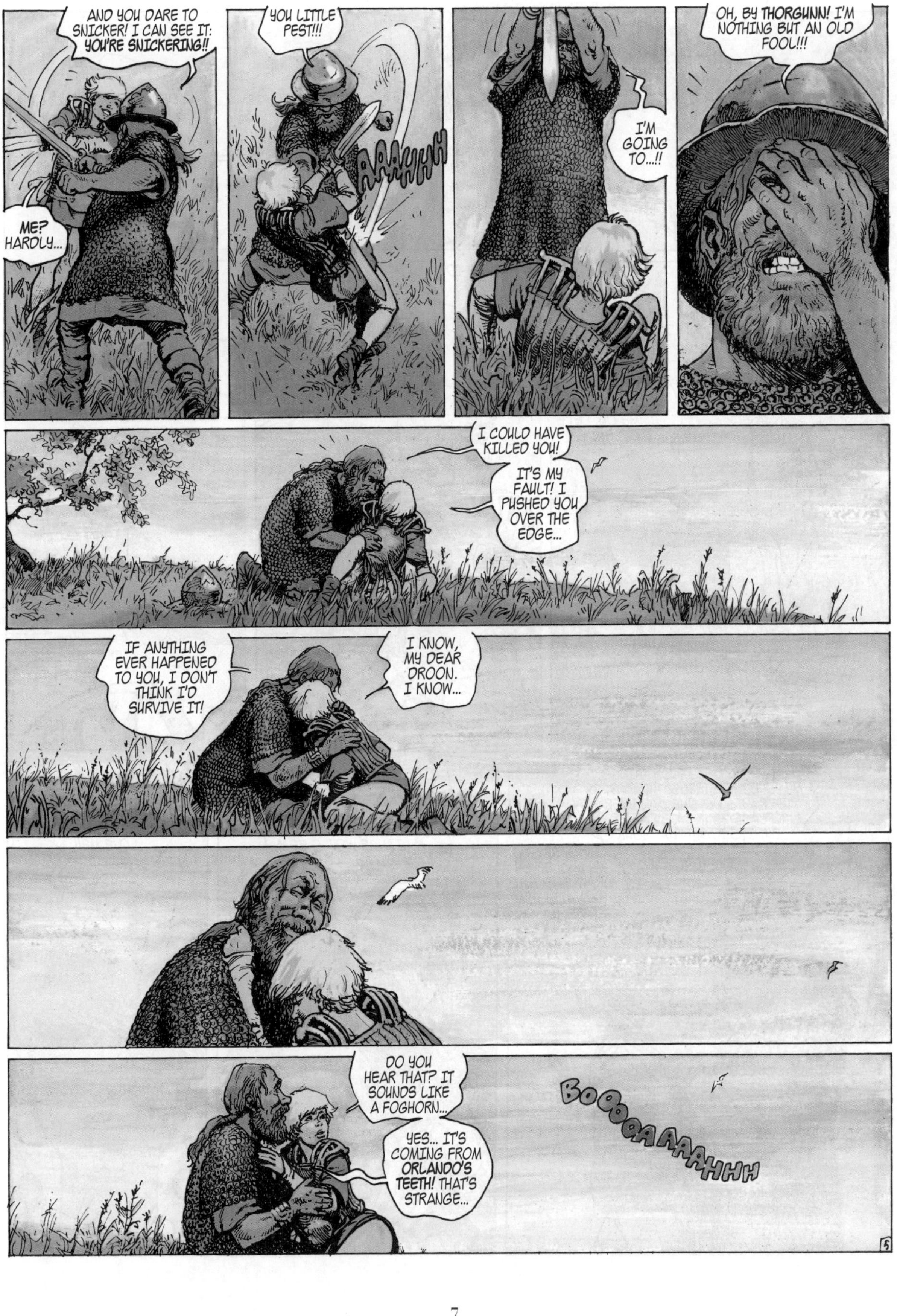
AND YOU DARE TO SNICKER! I CAN SEE IT: YOU'RE SNICKERING!!
ME? HARDLY...
YOU LITTLE PEST!!!
AAAHHH
I'M GOING TO...!!
OH, BY THORGUNN! I'M NOTHING BUT AN OLD FOOL!!!
I COULD HAVE KILLED YOU!
IT'S MY FAULT! I PUSHED YOU OVER THE EDGE...
IF ANYTHING EVER HAPPENED TO YOU, I DON'T THINK I'D SURVIVE IT!
I KNOW, MY DEAR DROON. I KNOW...
DO YOU HEAR THAT? IT SOUNDS LIKE A FOGHORN...
YES... IT'S COMING FROM ORLANDO'S TEETH! THAT'S STRANGE...
BOOOOAAAAHHHH
5

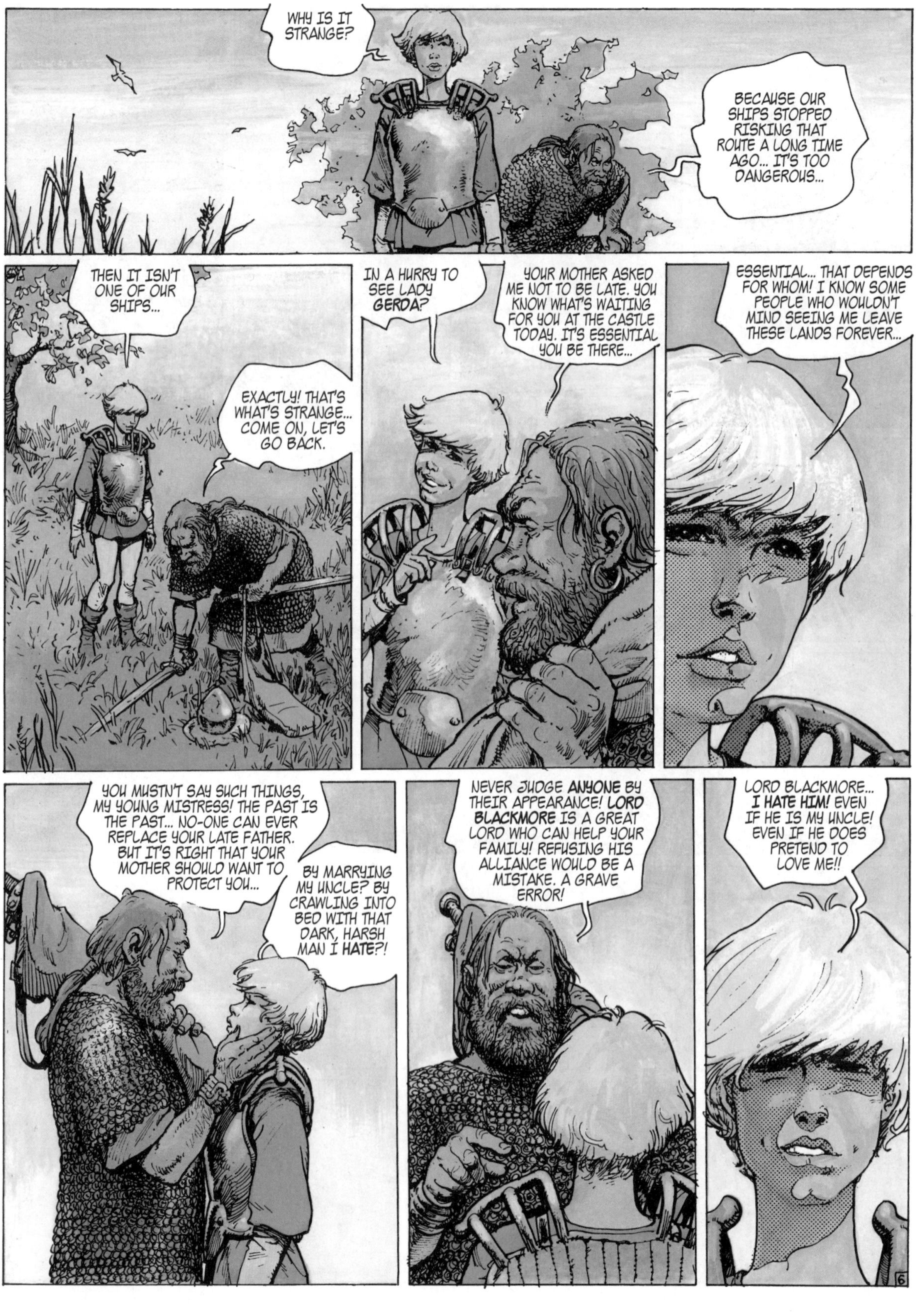

WHY IS IT STRANGE?
BECAUSE OUR SHIPS STOPPED RISKING THAT ROUTE A LONG TIME AGO... IT'S TOO DANGEROUS...
THEN IT ISN'T ONE OF OUR SHIPS...
EXACTLY! THAT'S WHAT'S STRANGE... COME ON, LET'S GO BACK.
IN A HURRY TO SEE LADY GERDA?
YOUR MOTHER ASKED ME NOT TO BE LATE. YOU KNOW WHAT'S WAITING FOR YOU AT THE CASTLE TODAY. IT'S ESSENTIAL YOU BE THERE...
ESSENTIAL... THAT DEPENDS FOR WHOM! I KNOW SOME PEOPLE WHO WOULDN'T MIND SEEING ME LEAVE THESE LANDS FOREVER...
YOU MUSTN'T SAY SUCH THINGS, MY YOUNG MISTRESS! THE PAST IS THE PAST... NO-ONE CAN EVER REPLACE YOUR LATE FATHER. BUT IT'S RIGHT THAT YOUR MOTHER SHOULD WANT TO PROTECT YOU...
BY MARRYING MY UNCLE? BY CRAWLING INTO BED WITH THAT DARK, HARSH MAN I HATE?!
NEVER JUDGE ANYONE BY THEIR APPEARANCE! LORD BLACKMORE IS A GREAT LORD WHO CAN HELP YOUR FAMILY! REFUSING HIS ALLIANCE WOULD BE A MISTAKE. A GRAVE ERROR!
LORD BLACKMORE... I HATE HIM! EVEN IF HE IS MY UNCLE! EVEN IF HE DOES PRETEND TO LOVE ME!!
6

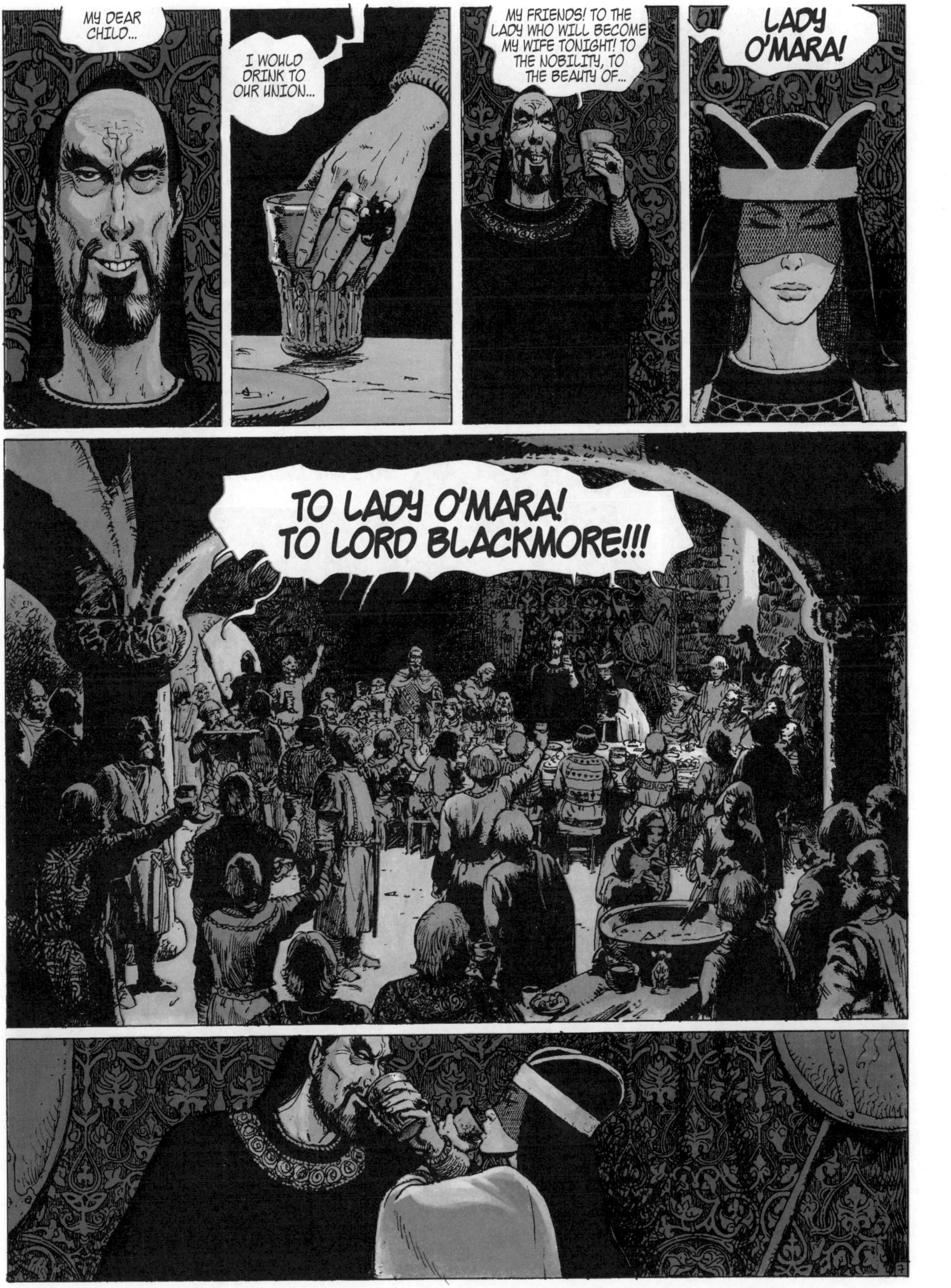
MY DEAR CHILD...
I WOULD DRINK TO OUR UNION...
MY FRIENDS! TO THE LADY WHO WILL BECOME MY WIFE TONIGHT! TO THE NOBILITY, TO THE BEAUTY OF...
LADY O'MARA!
TO LADY O'MARA! TO LORD BLACKMORE!!!

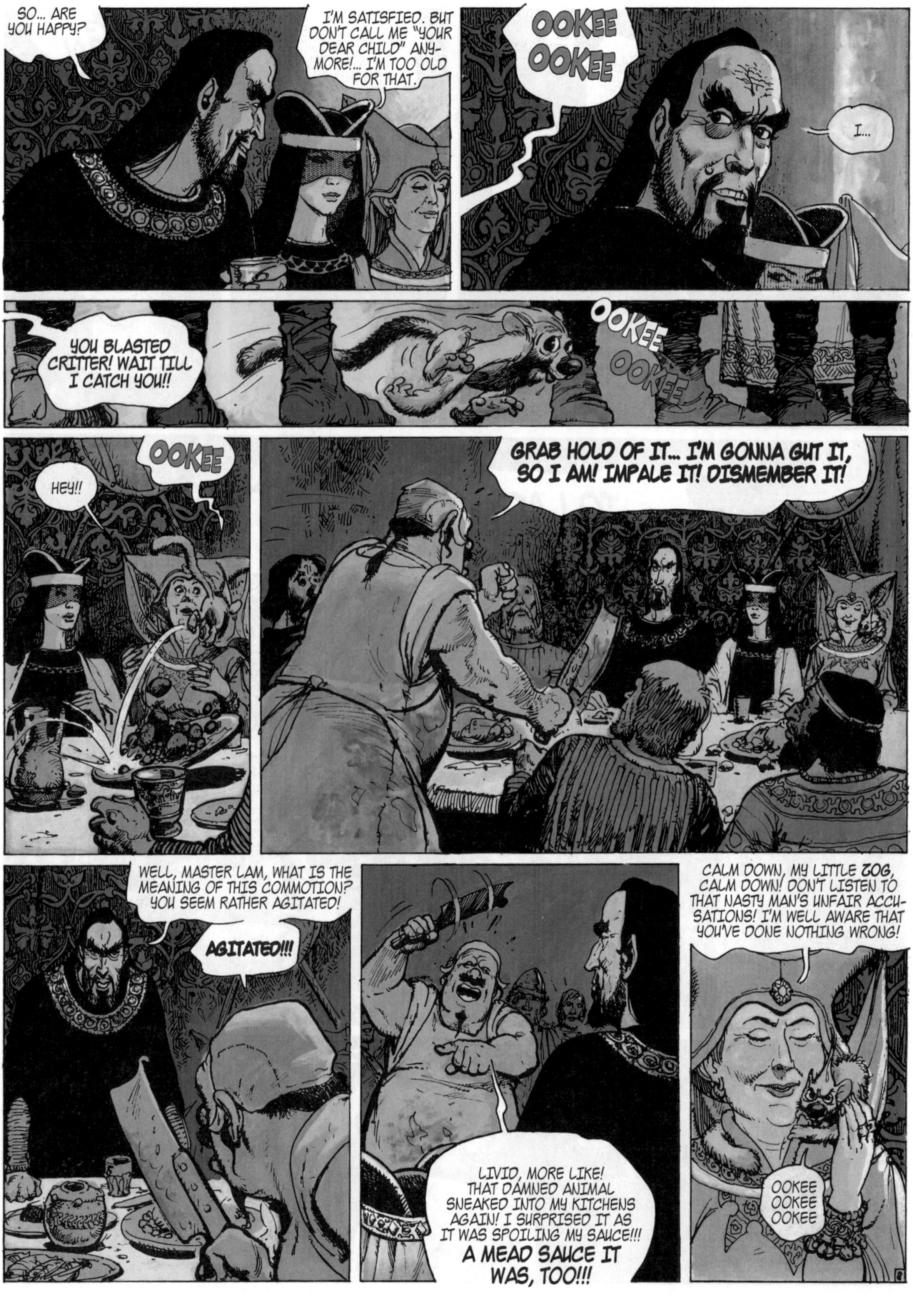

SO... ARE YOU HAPPY?
I'M SATISFIED. BUT DON'T CALL ME "YOUR DEAR CHILD" ANY-MORE!... I'M TOO OLD FOR THAT.
OOKEE OOKEE
I...
YOU BLASTED CRITTER! WAIT TILL I CATCH YOU!!
OOKEE OOKEE
OOKEE
HEY!!
GRAB HOLD OF IT... I'M GONNA GUT IT, SO I AM! IMPALE IT! DISMEMBER IT!
WELL, MASTER LAM, WHAT IS THE MEANING OF THIS COMMOTION? YOU SEEM RATHER AGITATED!
AGITATED!!!
LIVID, MORE LIKE! THAT DAMNED ANIMAL SNEAKED INTO MY KITCHENS AGAIN! I SURPRISED IT AS IT WAS SPOILING MY SAUCE!!!
A MEAD SAUCE IT WAS, TOO!!!
CALM DOWN, MY LITTLE ZOG, CALM DOWN! DON'T LISTEN TO THAT NASTY MAN'S UNFAIR ACCU-SATIONS! I'M WELL AWARE THAT YOU'VE DONE NOTHING WRONG!
OOKEE OOKEE OOKEE
8

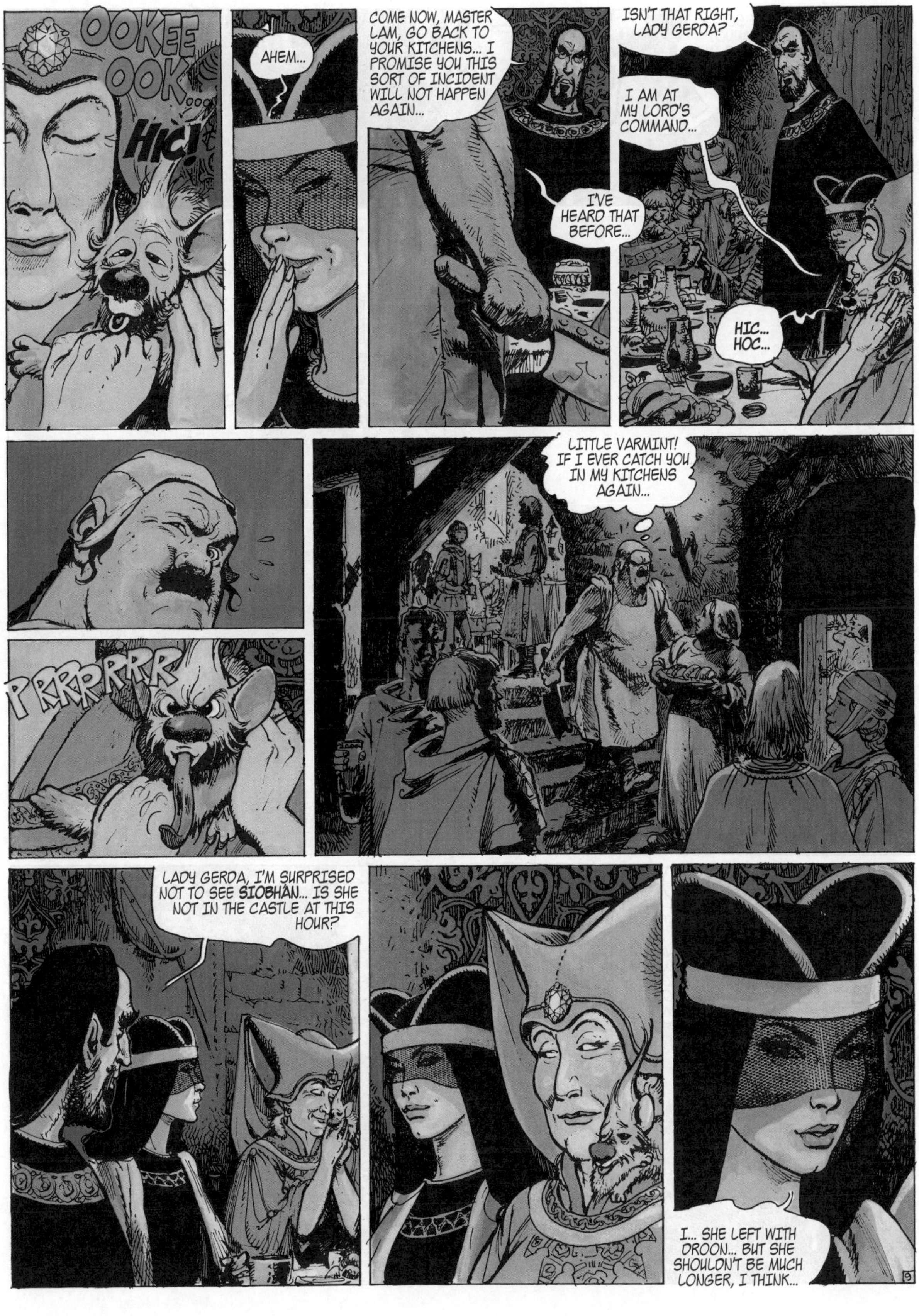
OOKEE OOK...
HIC!
AHEM...
COME NOW, MASTER LAM, GO BACK TO YOUR KITCHENS... I PROMISE YOU THIS SORT OF INCIDENT WILL NOT HAPPEN AGAIN...
I'VE HEARD THAT BEFORE...
ISN'T THAT RIGHT, LADY GERDA?
I AM AT MY LORD'S COMMAND...
HIC... HOC...
PRRRRRRR
LITTLE VARMINT! IF I EVER CATCH YOU IN MY KITCHENS AGAIN...
LADY GERDA, I'M SURPRISED NOT TO SEE SIOBHAN... IS SHE NOT IN THE CASTLE AT THIS HOUR?
I... SHE LEFT WITH DROON... BUT SHE SHOULDN'T BE MUCH LONGER, I THINK...
3

BUT... I HOPE SO, MY DEAR... I CANNOT WAIT TO HOLD HER IN MY ARMS... THAT CHILD... WHO WILL SOON BE OURS!

DROON, YOU DIDN'T ANSWER ME WHEN I ASKED YOU WHAT THE **LAMENT OF THE LOST MOORS** WAS...

IT'S AN OLD LEGEND... SO OLD THAT FEW EVEN REMEMBER IT ANYMORE...

... EXCEPT FOR OLD FOLKS LIKE YOU AND LADY GERDA!

OI! EASY, YOUNG LADY! OLD I AM NOT, NEITHER IN SOUL NOR IN VIGOUR — YOU SHOULD KNOW IT!

MISTRESS... HURRY! THE CELE-BRATIONS HAVE BEGUN! YOU'RE THE LAST ONE TO ARRIVE...

DARN!

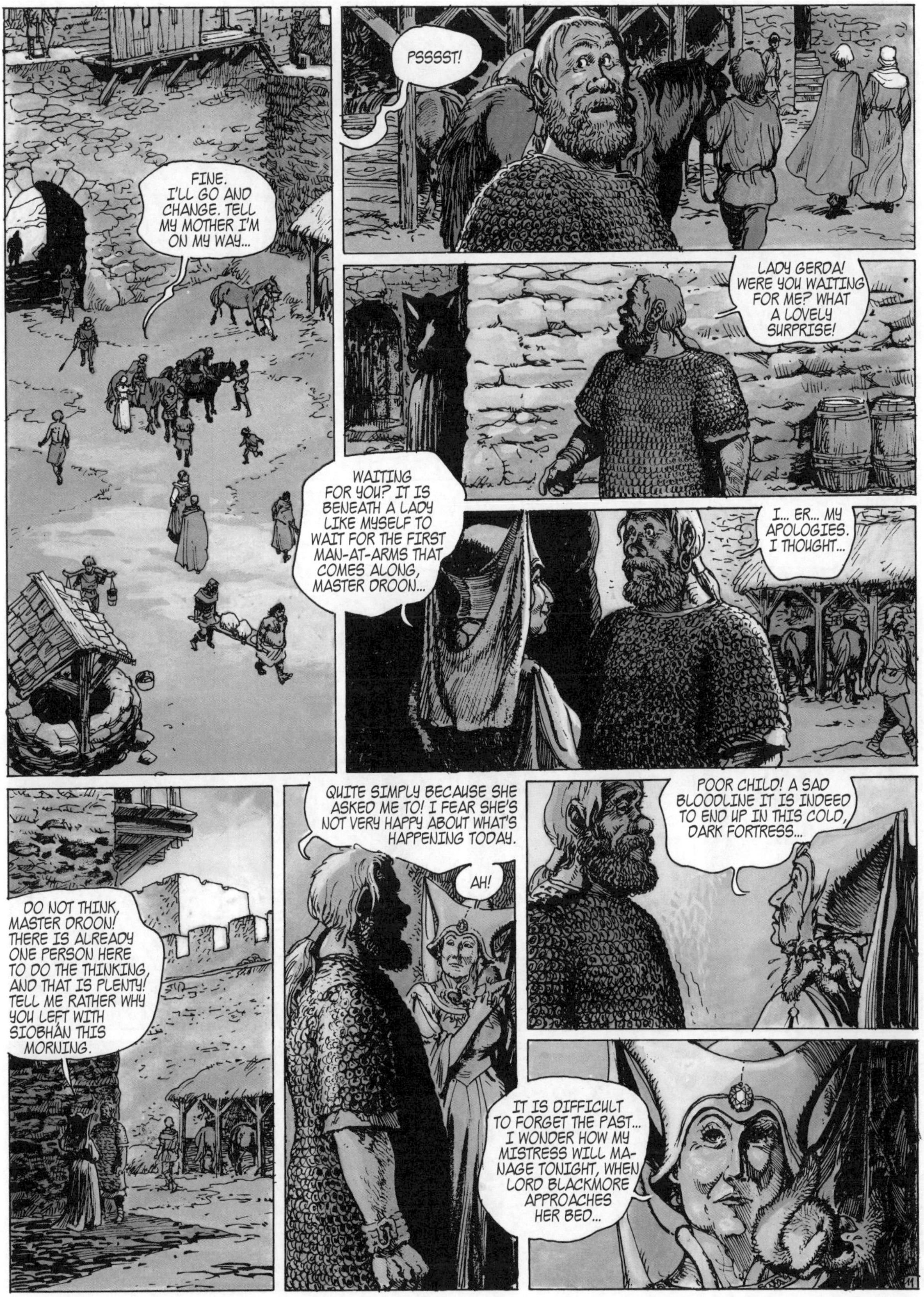
FINE. I'LL GO AND CHANGE. TELL MY MOTHER I'M ON MY WAY...
PSSSST!
LADY GERDA! WERE YOU WAITING FOR ME? WHAT A LOVELY SURPRISE!
WAITING FOR YOU? IT IS BENEATH A LADY LIKE MYSELF TO WAIT FOR THE FIRST MAN-AT-ARMS THAT COMES ALONG, MASTER DROON...
I... ER... MY APOLOGIES. I THOUGHT...
DO NOT THINK, MASTER DROON! THERE IS ALREADY ONE PERSON HERE TO DO THE THINKING, AND THAT IS PLENTY! TELL ME RATHER WHY YOU LEFT WITH SIOBHÁN THIS MORNING.
QUITE SIMPLY BECAUSE SHE ASKED ME TO! I FEAR SHE'S NOT VERY HAPPY ABOUT WHAT'S HAPPENING TODAY.
AH!
POOR CHILD! A SAD BLOODLINE IT IS INDEED TO END UP IN THIS COLD, DARK FORTRESS...
IT IS DIFFICULT TO FORGET THE PAST... I WONDER HOW MY MISTRESS WILL MANAGE TONIGHT, WHEN LORD BLACKMORE APPROACHES HER BED...
11

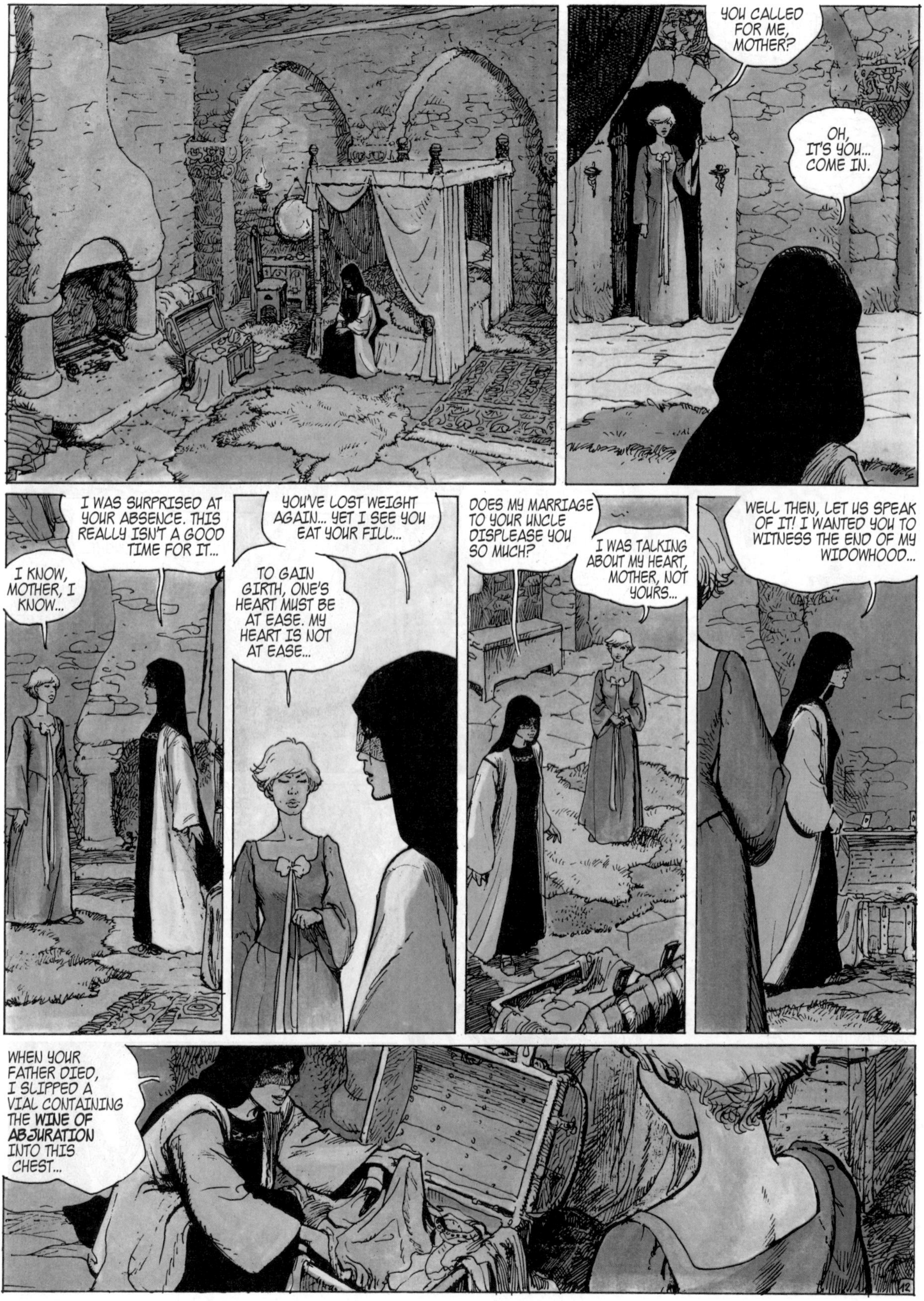
YOU CALLED FOR ME, MOTHER?
OH, IT'S YOU... COME IN.
I WAS SURPRISED AT YOUR ABSENCE. THIS REALLY ISN'T A GOOD TIME FOR IT...
I KNOW, MOTHER, I KNOW...
YOU'VE LOST WEIGHT AGAIN... YET I SEE YOU EAT YOUR FILL...
TO GAIN GIRTH, ONE'S HEART MUST BE AT EASE. MY HEART IS NOT AT EASE...
DOES MY MARRIAGE TO YOUR UNCLE DISPLEASE YOU SO MUCH?
I WAS TALKING ABOUT MY HEART, MOTHER, NOT YOURS...
WELL THEN, LET US SPEAK OF IT! I WANTED YOU TO WITNESS THE END OF MY WIDOWHOOD...
WHEN YOUR FATHER DIED, I SLIPPED A VIAL CONTAINING THE WINE OF ABJURATION INTO THIS CHEST...
12

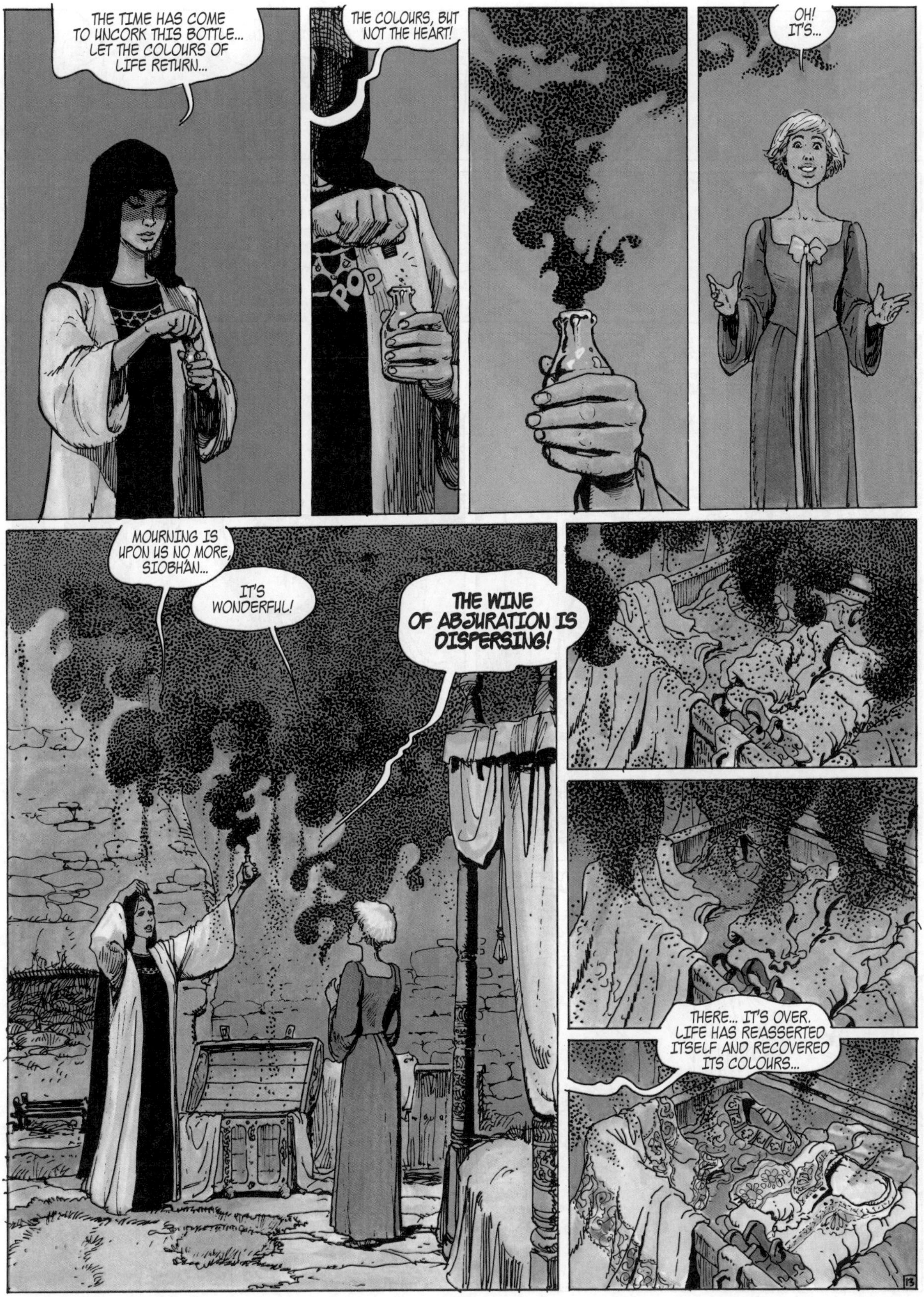
THE TIME HAS COME TO UNCORK THIS BOTTLE... LET THE COLOURS OF LIFE RETURN...
THE COLOURS, BUT NOT THE HEART!
POP
OH! IT'S...
MOURNING IS UPON US NO MORE, SIOBHÁN...
IT'S WONDERFUL!
THE WINE OF ABJURATION IS DISPERSING!
THERE... IT'S OVER. LIFE HAS REASSERTED ITSELF AND RECOVERED ITS COLOURS...
13

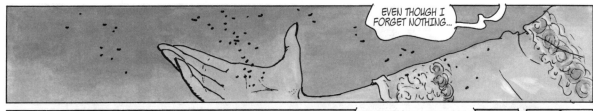

EVEN THOUGH I FORGET NOTHING...

EVEN THOUGH MY HEART SHALL NEVER AGAIN BEAT AS BEFORE!

SO, HOW DO YOU FIND ME NOW? IT'S MUCH MORE CHEERFUL LIKE THIS, ISN'T IT?

OH, MUMMY! YOU'RE SO BEAUTIFUL! AND HOW I WISH YOU COULD BE HAPPY...

MUMMY, WHILE I WAS WITH DROON THIS MORNING, I HEARD A FOGHORN THAT SEEMED TO COME FROM ORLANDO'S TEETH...

THAT HORN SHOOK MY SOUL...

IT WAS AS IF SOMEONE WAS CALLING OUT TO ME...

...AS IF FATHER WERE COMING FOR US.

A FOGHORN... IN ORLANDO'S PASSAGE! HOW STRANGE THAT IS, MY DAUGHTER...

16

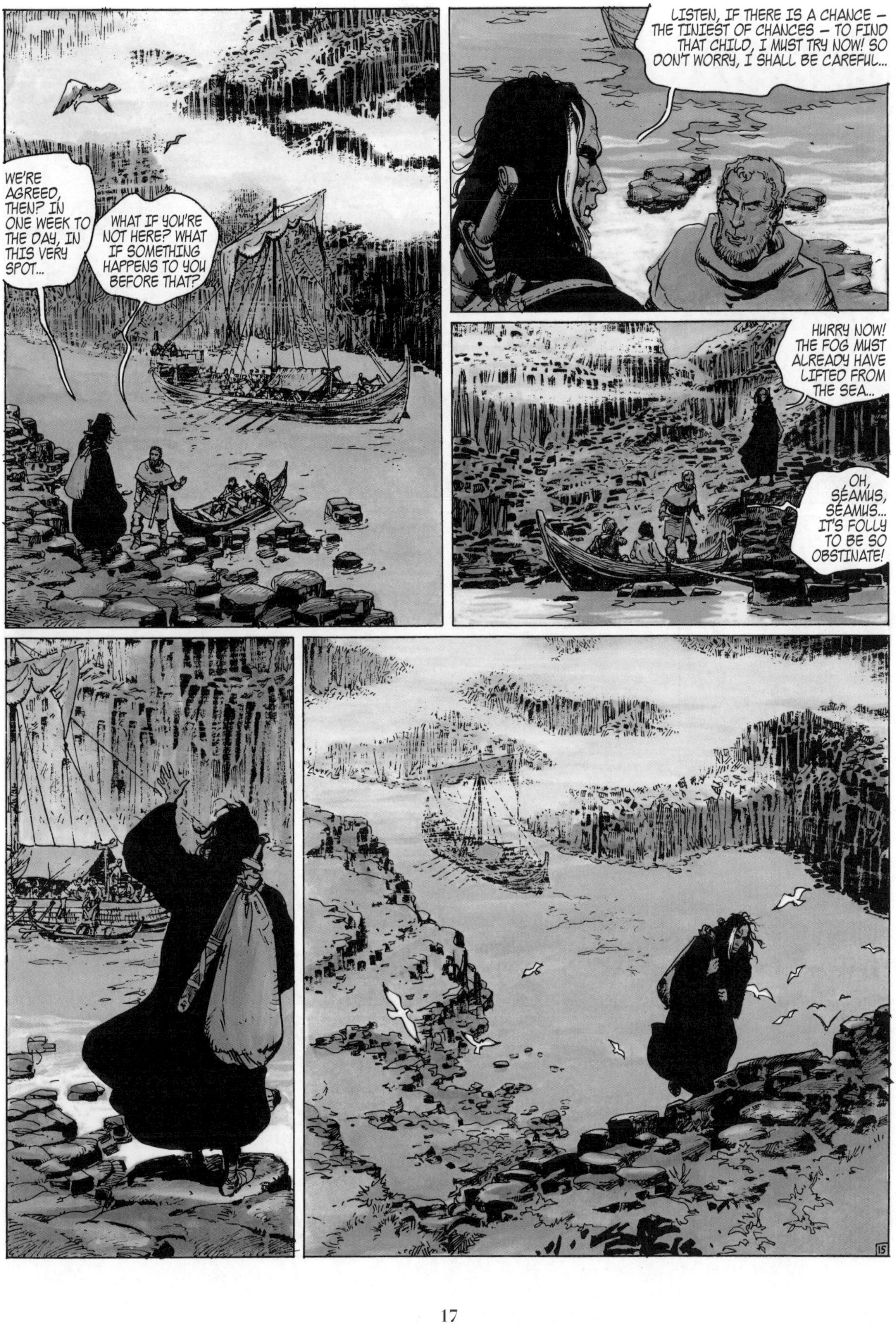
WE'RE AGREED, THEN? IN ONE WEEK TO THE DAY, IN THIS VERY SPOT...
WHAT IF YOU'RE NOT HERE? WHAT IF SOMETHING HAPPENS TO YOU BEFORE THAT?
LISTEN, IF THERE IS A CHANCE – THE TINIEST OF CHANCES – TO FIND THAT CHILD, I MUST TRY NOW! SO DON'T WORRY, I SHALL BE CAREFUL...
HURRY NOW! THE FOG MUST ALREADY HAVE LIFTED FROM THE SEA...
OH, SÉAMUS, SÉAMUS... IT'S FOLLY TO BE SO OBSTINATE!
15

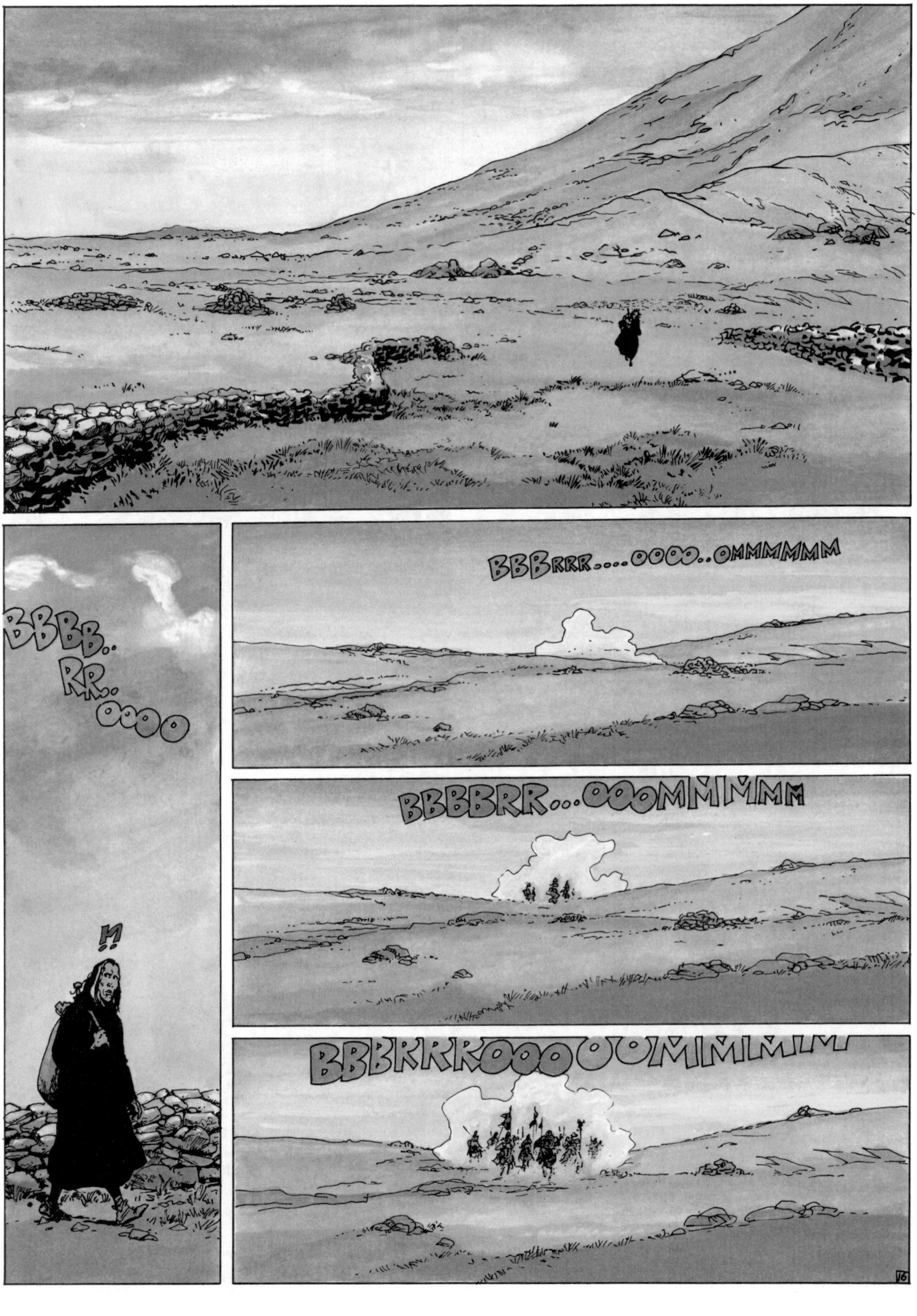
BBBB..
RR..
OOOO
!?
BBBRRR....OOOO..OMMMMMM
BBBBRR...OOOMMMMM
BBBRRROOOOOMMMMM
16

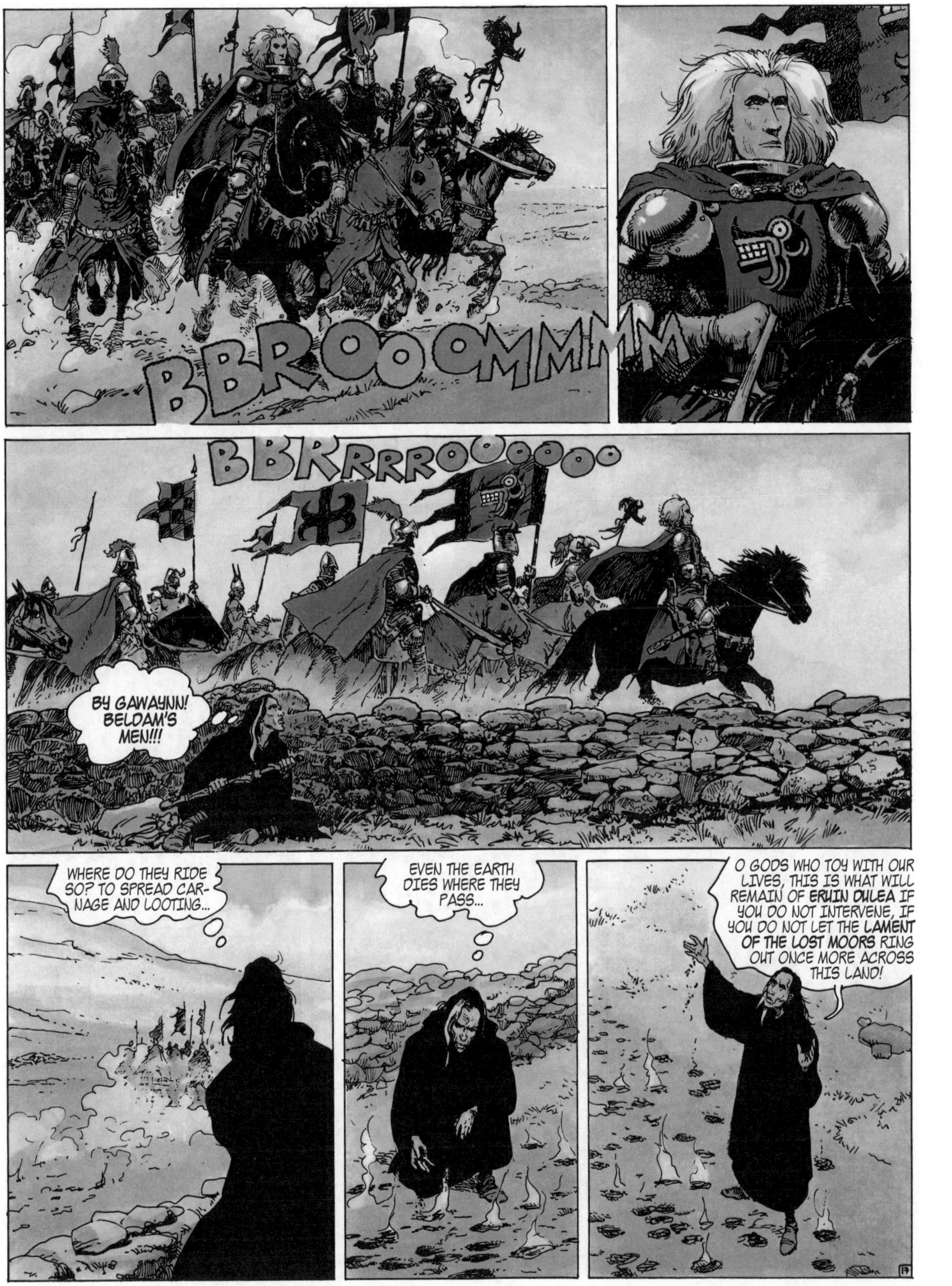
BBROOOMMMM
BBRRRROOOOOOO
BY GAWAYNN! BELDAM'S MEN!!!
WHERE DO THEY RIDE SO? TO SPREAD CAR-NAGE AND LOOTING...
EVEN THE EARTH DIES WHERE THEY PASS...
O GODS WHO TOY WITH OUR LIVES, THIS IS WHAT WILL REMAIN OF **ERUIN DULEA** IF YOU DO NOT INTERVENE, IF YOU DO NOT LET THE **LAMENT OF THE LOST MOORS** RING OUT ONCE MORE ACROSS THIS LAND!
17

FROM GODS TO MEN, NEVER SHALL THE LINE BE BROKEN!
FROM GODS TO MEN, NEVER SHALL THE LINE BE BROKEN!
MEN REQUIRE PROTECTION. GODS DEMAND FAITHFULNESS. MAY THE FAITHFULNESS OF EACH BE THE FAITHFULNESS OF ALL...
MAY THE FAITHFULNESS OF LADY O'MARA BE THE FAITHFULNESS OF LORD BLACKMORE. MAY THE FAITHFULNESS OF LORD BLACKMORE BE THE FAITHFULNESS OF LADY O'MARA!
MAY THE ONE'S BLOOD BECOME THE OTHER'S.

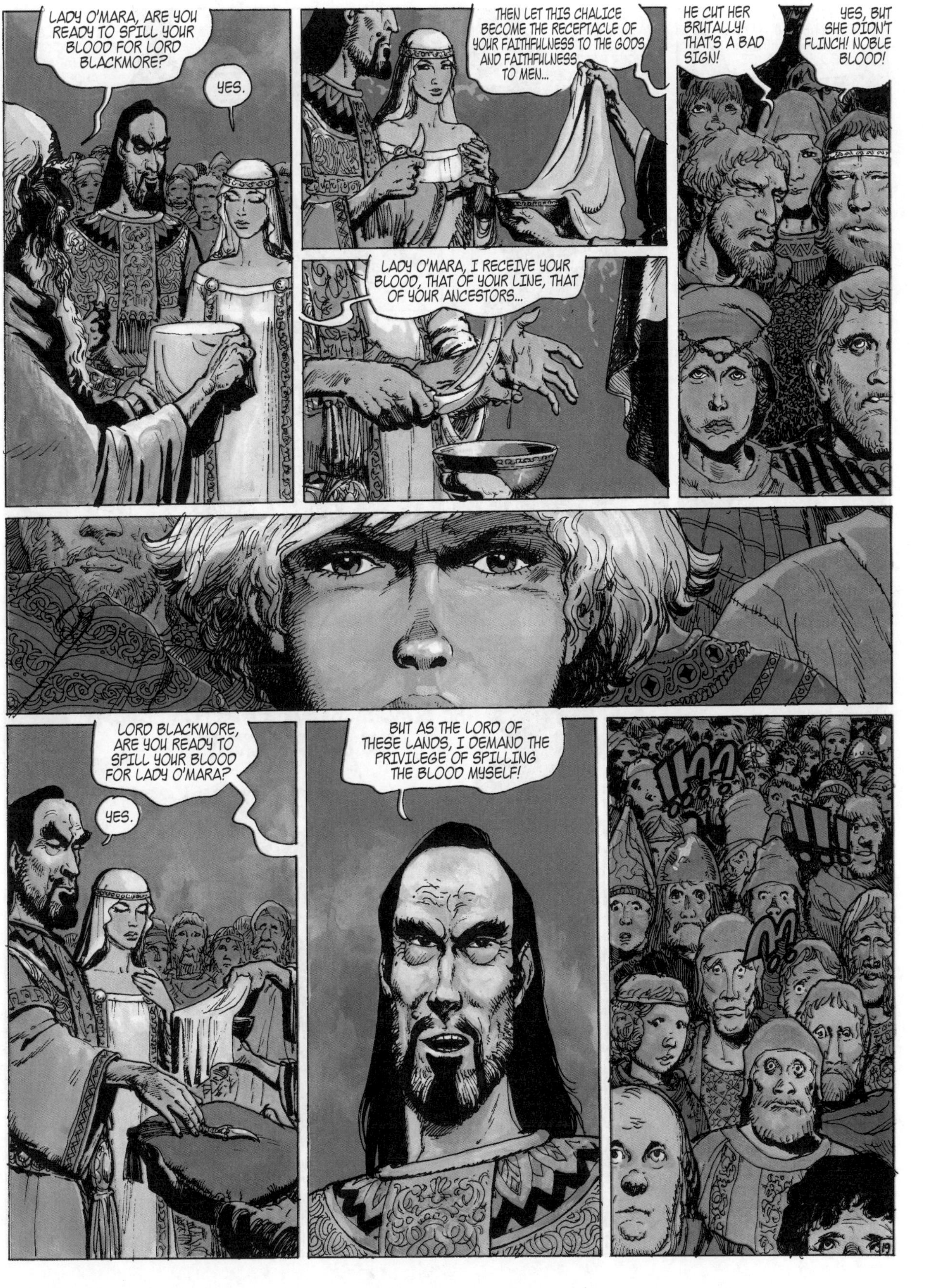

LADY O'MARA, ARE YOU READY TO SPILL YOUR BLOOD FOR LORD BLACKMORE?
YES.
THEN LET THIS CHALICE BECOME THE RECEPTACLE OF YOUR FAITHFULNESS TO THE GODS AND FAITHFULNESS TO MEN...
LADY O'MARA, I RECEIVE YOUR BLOOD, THAT OF YOUR LINE, THAT OF YOUR ANCESTORS...
HE CUT HER BRUTALLY! THAT'S A BAD SIGN!
YES, BUT SHE DIDN'T FLINCH! NOBLE BLOOD!
LORD BLACKMORE, ARE YOU READY TO SPILL YOUR BLOOD FOR LADY O'MARA?
YES.
BUT AS THE LORD OF THESE LANDS, I DEMAND THE PRIVILEGE OF SPILLING THE BLOOD MYSELF!

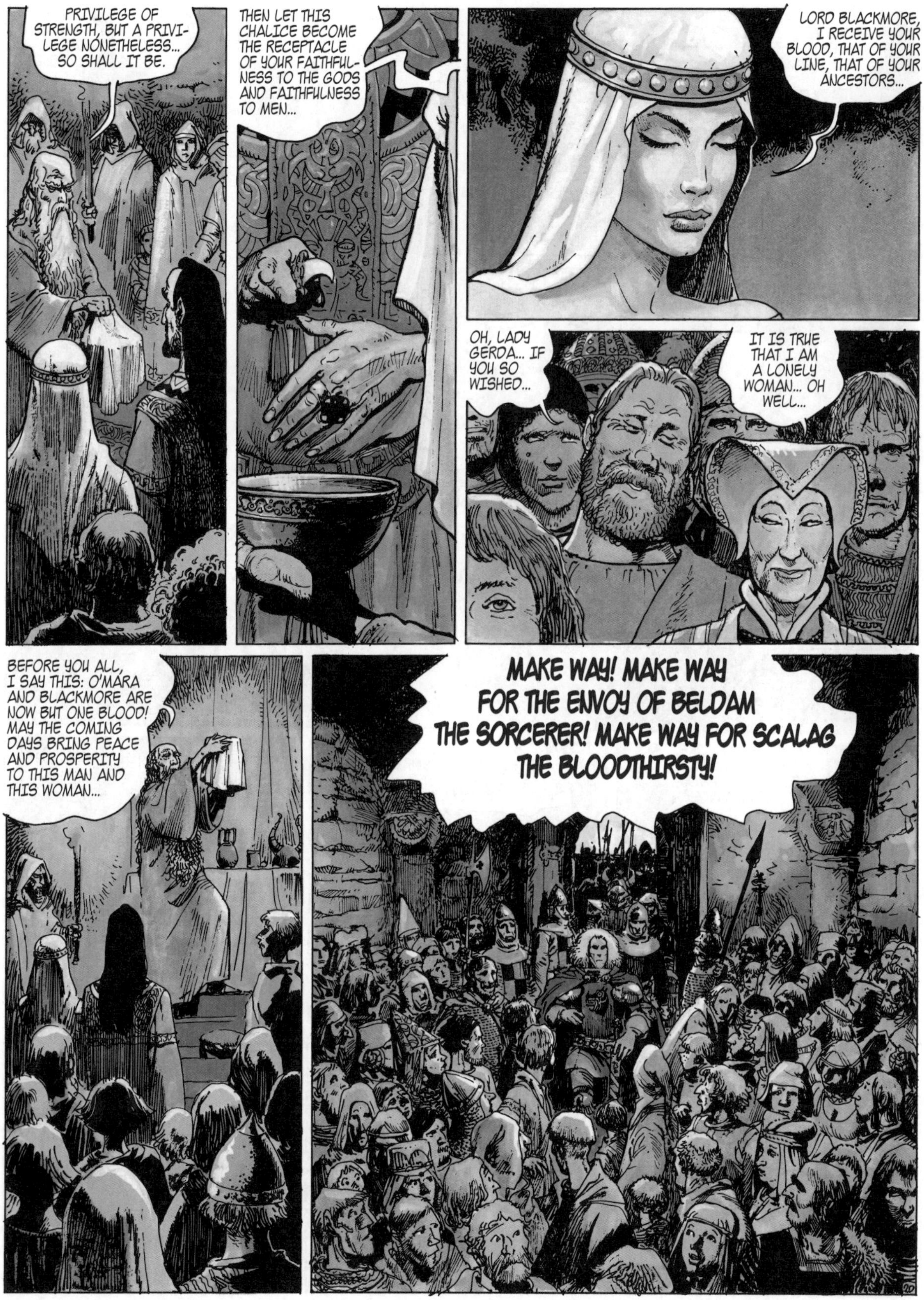
PRIVILEGE OF STRENGTH, BUT A PRIVI-LEGE NONETHELESS... SO SHALL IT BE.
THEN LET THIS CHALICE BECOME THE RECEPTACLE OF YOUR FAITHFUL-NESS TO THE GODS AND FAITHFULNESS TO MEN...
LORD BLACKMORE, I RECEIVE YOUR BLOOD, THAT OF YOUR LINE, THAT OF YOUR ANCESTORS...
OH, LADY GERDA... IF YOU SO WISHED...
IT IS TRUE THAT I AM A LONELY WOMAN... OH WELL...
BEFORE YOU ALL, I SAY THIS: O'MARA AND BLACKMORE ARE NOW BUT ONE BLOOD! MAY THE COMING DAYS BRING PEACE AND PROSPERITY TO THIS MAN AND THIS WOMAN...
MAKE WAY! MAKE WAY FOR THE ENVOY OF BELDAM THE SORCERER! MAKE WAY FOR SCALAG THE BLOODTHIRSTY!

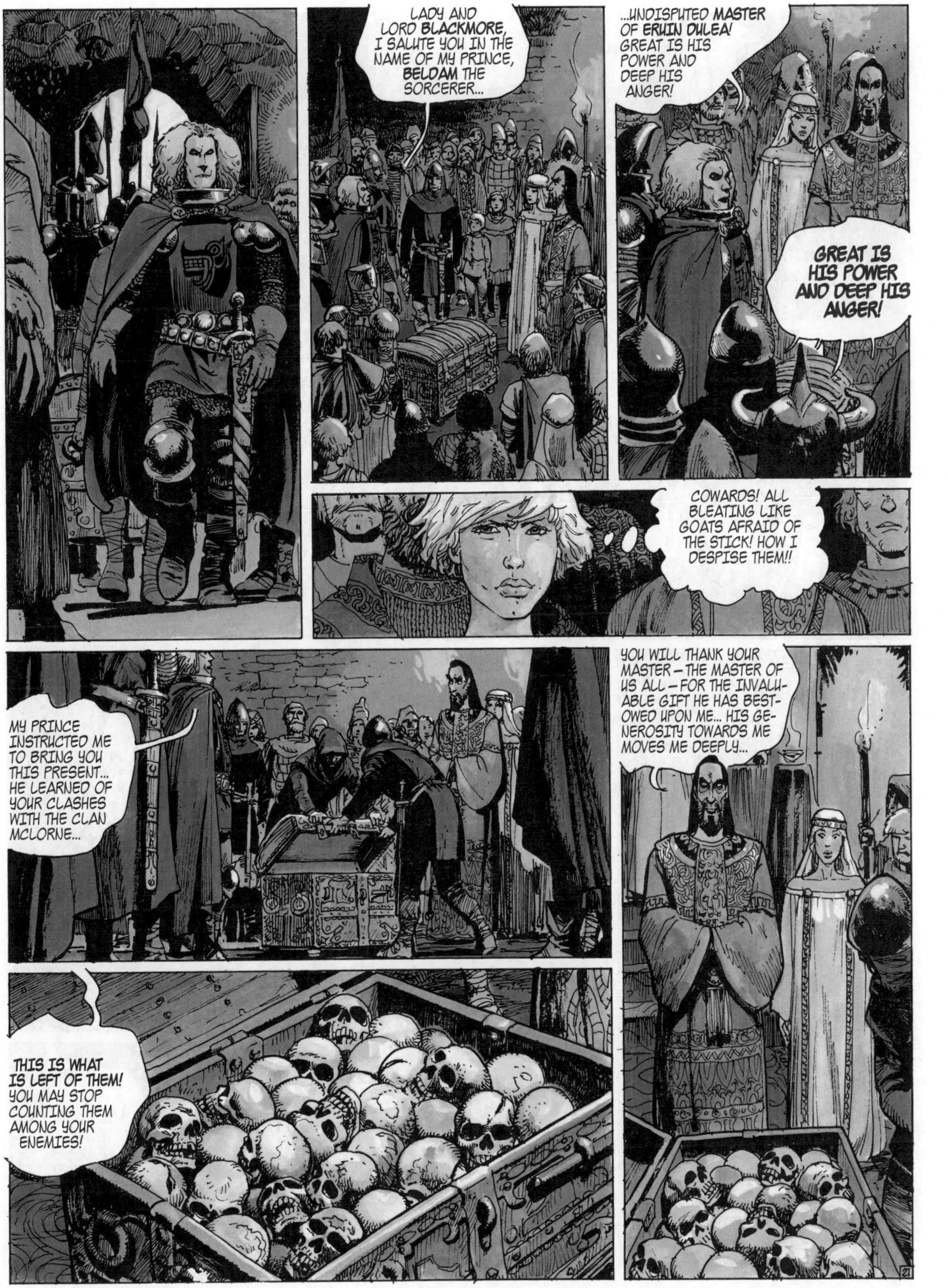
LADY AND LORD BLACKMORE, I SALUTE YOU IN THE NAME OF MY PRINCE, BELDAM THE SORCERER...
...UNDISPUTED MASTER OF ERVIN DULEA! GREAT IS HIS POWER AND DEEP HIS ANGER!
GREAT IS HIS POWER AND DEEP HIS ANGER!
COWARDS! ALL BLEATING LIKE GOATS AFRAID OF THE STICK! HOW I DESPISE THEM!!
MY PRINCE INSTRUCTED ME TO BRING YOU THIS PRESENT... HE LEARNED OF YOUR CLASHES WITH THE CLAN MCLORNE...
THIS IS WHAT IS LEFT OF THEM! YOU MAY STOP COUNTING THEM AMONG YOUR ENEMIES!
YOU WILL THANK YOUR MASTER – THE MASTER OF US ALL – FOR THE INVALUABLE GIFT HE HAS BESTOWED UPON ME... HIS GENEROSITY TOWARDS ME MOVES ME DEEPLY...
21

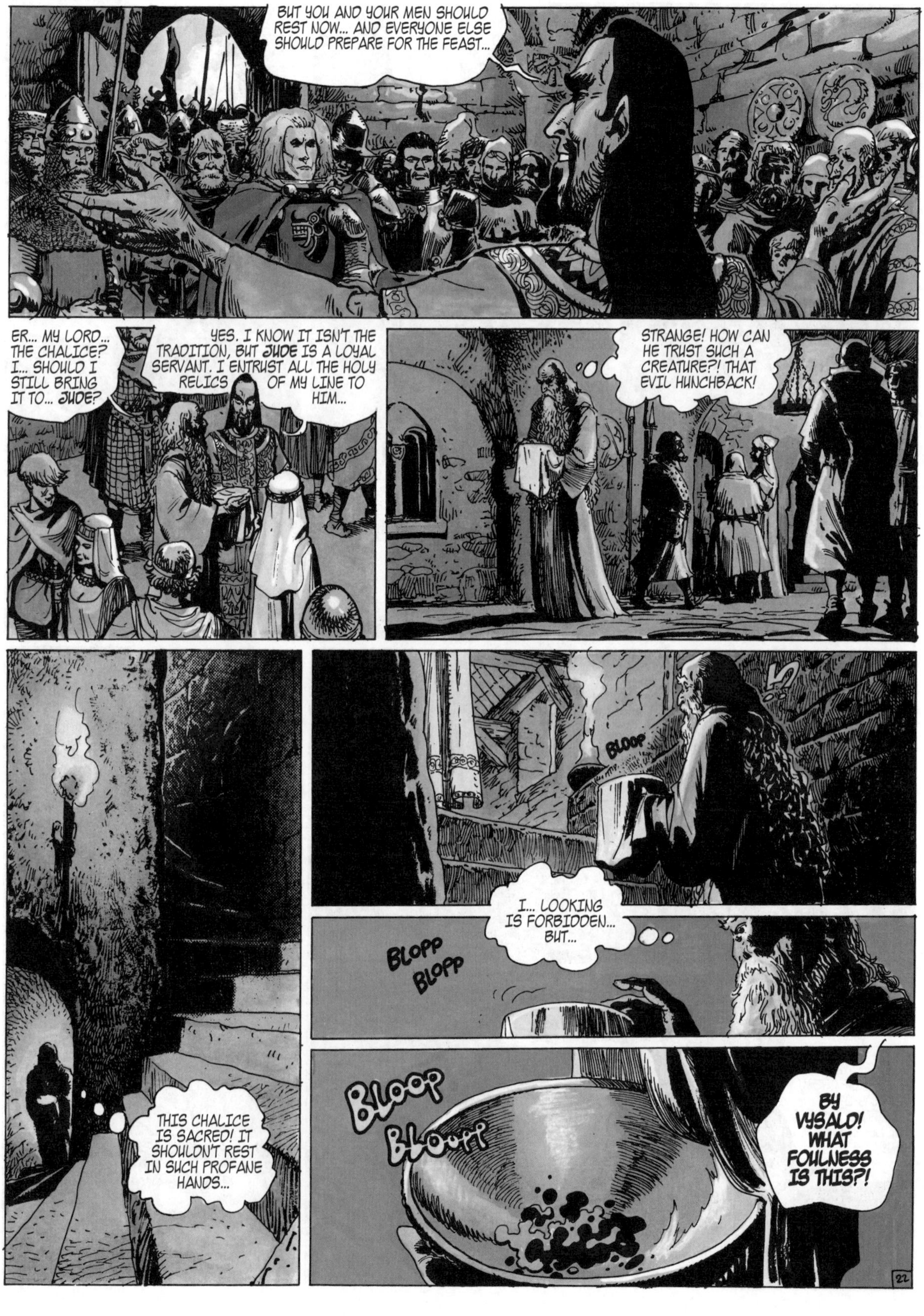
BUT YOU AND YOUR MEN SHOULD REST NOW... AND EVERYONE ELSE SHOULD PREPARE FOR THE FEAST...
ER... MY LORD... THE CHALICE? I... SHOULD I STILL BRING IT TO... JUDE?
YES. I KNOW IT ISN'T THE TRADITION, BUT JUDE IS A LOYAL SERVANT. I ENTRUST ALL THE HOLY RELICS OF MY LINE TO HIM...
STRANGE! HOW CAN HE TRUST SUCH A CREATURE?! THAT EVIL HUNCHBACK!
THIS CHALICE IS SACRED! IT SHOULDN'T REST IN SUCH PROFANE HANDS...
BLOOP
I... LOOKING IS FORBIDDEN... BUT...
BLOPP BLOPP
BLOOP BLOOPP
BY VYSALD! WHAT FOULNESS IS THIS?!
22

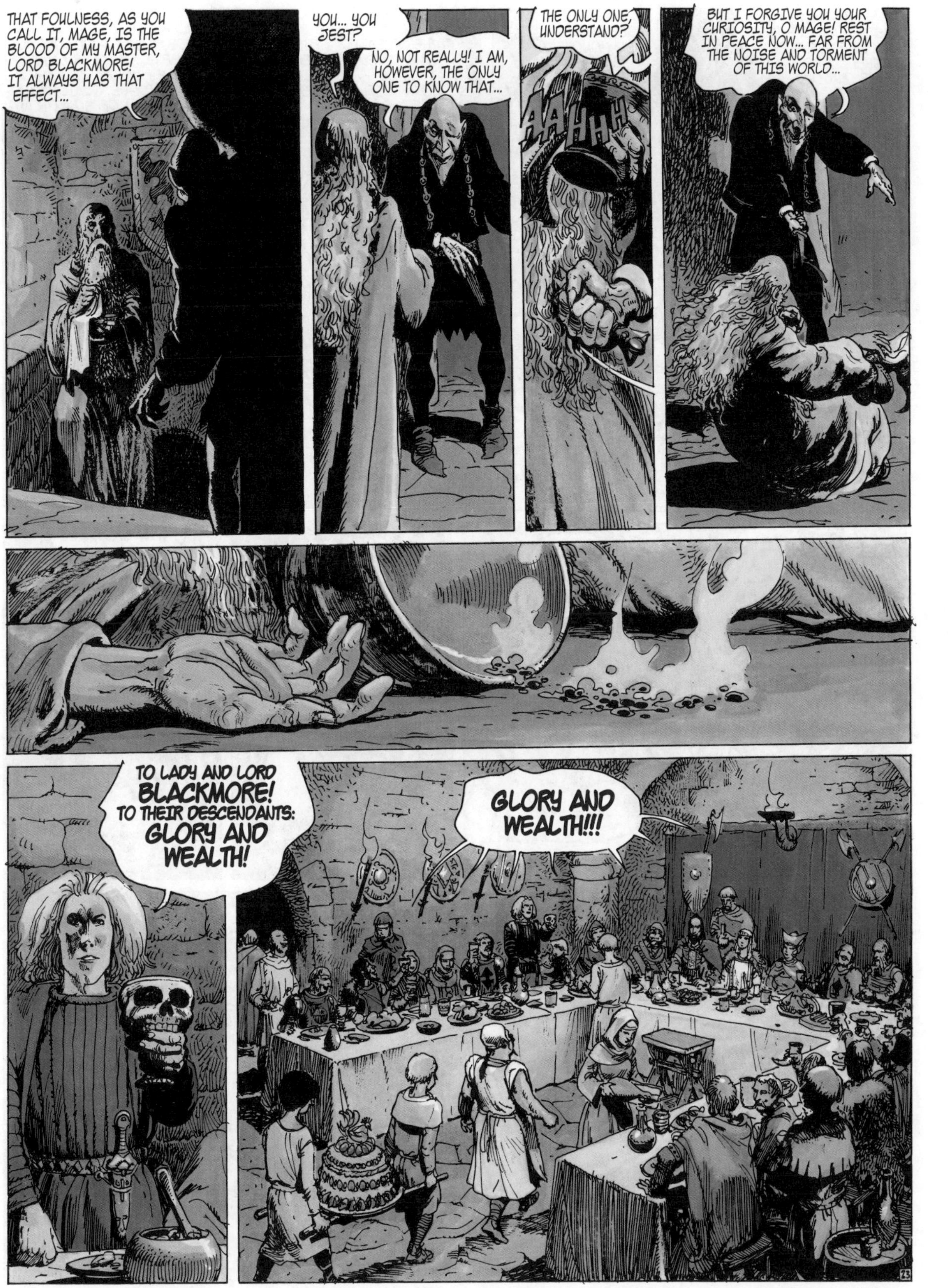
THAT FOULNESS, AS YOU CALL IT, MAGE, IS THE BLOOD OF MY MASTER, LORD BLACKMORE! IT ALWAYS HAS THAT EFFECT...
YOU... YOU JEST?
NO, NOT REALLY! I AM, HOWEVER, THE ONLY ONE TO KNOW THAT...
THE ONLY ONE, UNDERSTAND?
AAHHH
BUT I FORGIVE YOU YOUR CURIOSITY, O MAGE! REST IN PEACE NOW... FAR FROM THE NOISE AND TORMENT OF THIS WORLD...
TO LADY AND LORD BLACKMORE! TO THEIR DESCENDANTS: GLORY AND WEALTH!
GLORY AND WEALTH!!!
23

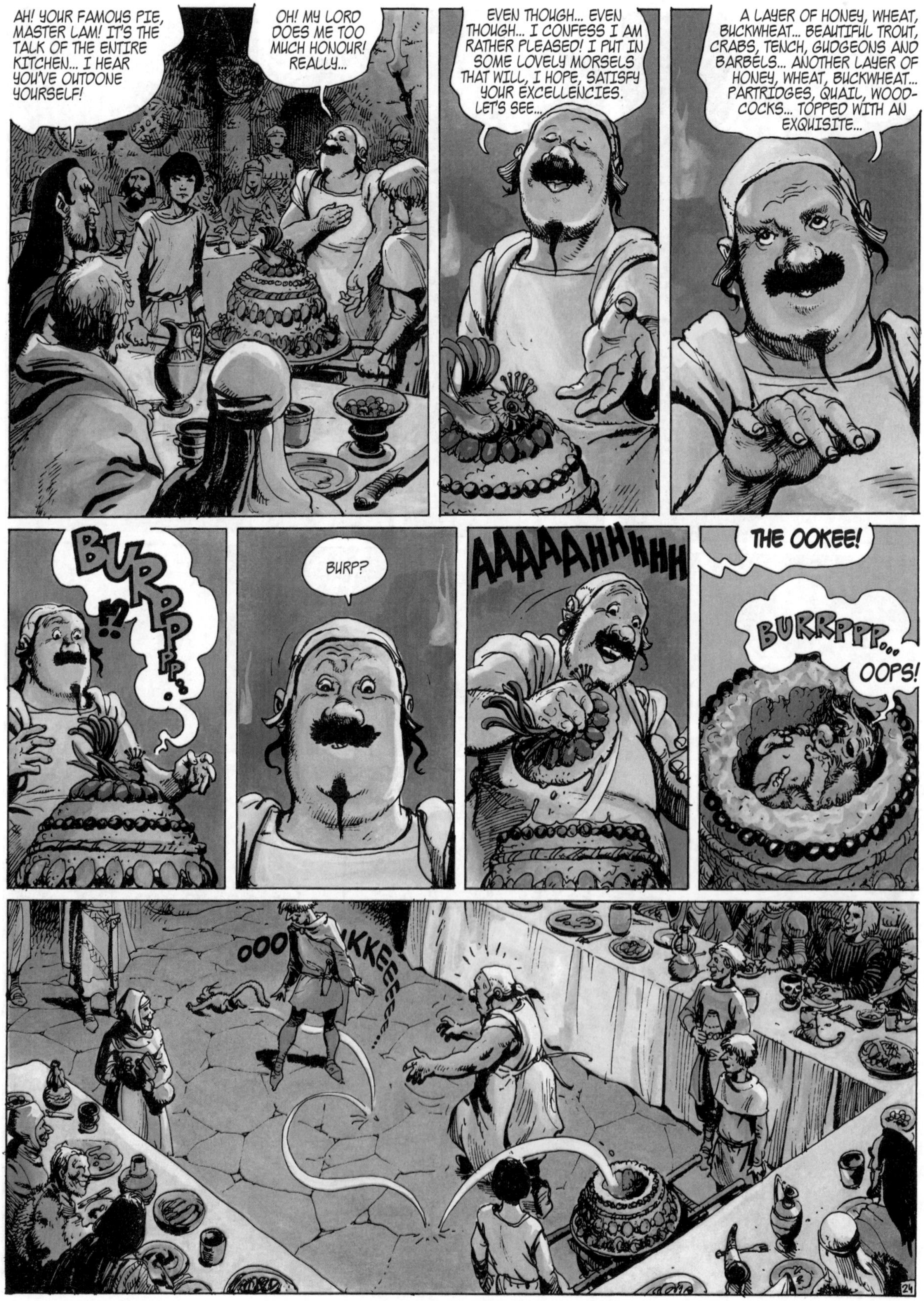

AH! YOUR FAMOUS PIE, MASTER LAM! IT'S THE TALK OF THE ENTIRE KITCHEN... I HEAR YOU'VE OUTDONE YOURSELF!
OH! MY LORD DOES ME TOO MUCH HONOUR! REALLY...
EVEN THOUGH... EVEN THOUGH... I CONFESS I AM RATHER PLEASED! I PUT IN SOME LOVELY MORSELS THAT WILL, I HOPE, SATISFY YOUR EXCELLENCIES. LET'S SEE...
A LAYER OF HONEY, WHEAT, BUCKWHEAT... BEAUTIFUL TROUT, CRABS, TENCH, GUDGEONS AND BARBELS... ANOTHER LAYER OF HONEY, WHEAT, BUCKWHEAT... PARTRIDGES, QUAIL, WOODCOCKS... TOPPED WITH AN EXQUISITE...
BURPPPP...
!?
BURP?
AAAAAHHHHHH
THE OOKEE!
BURRPPP...
OOPS!
OOO
IKKEEEEE...

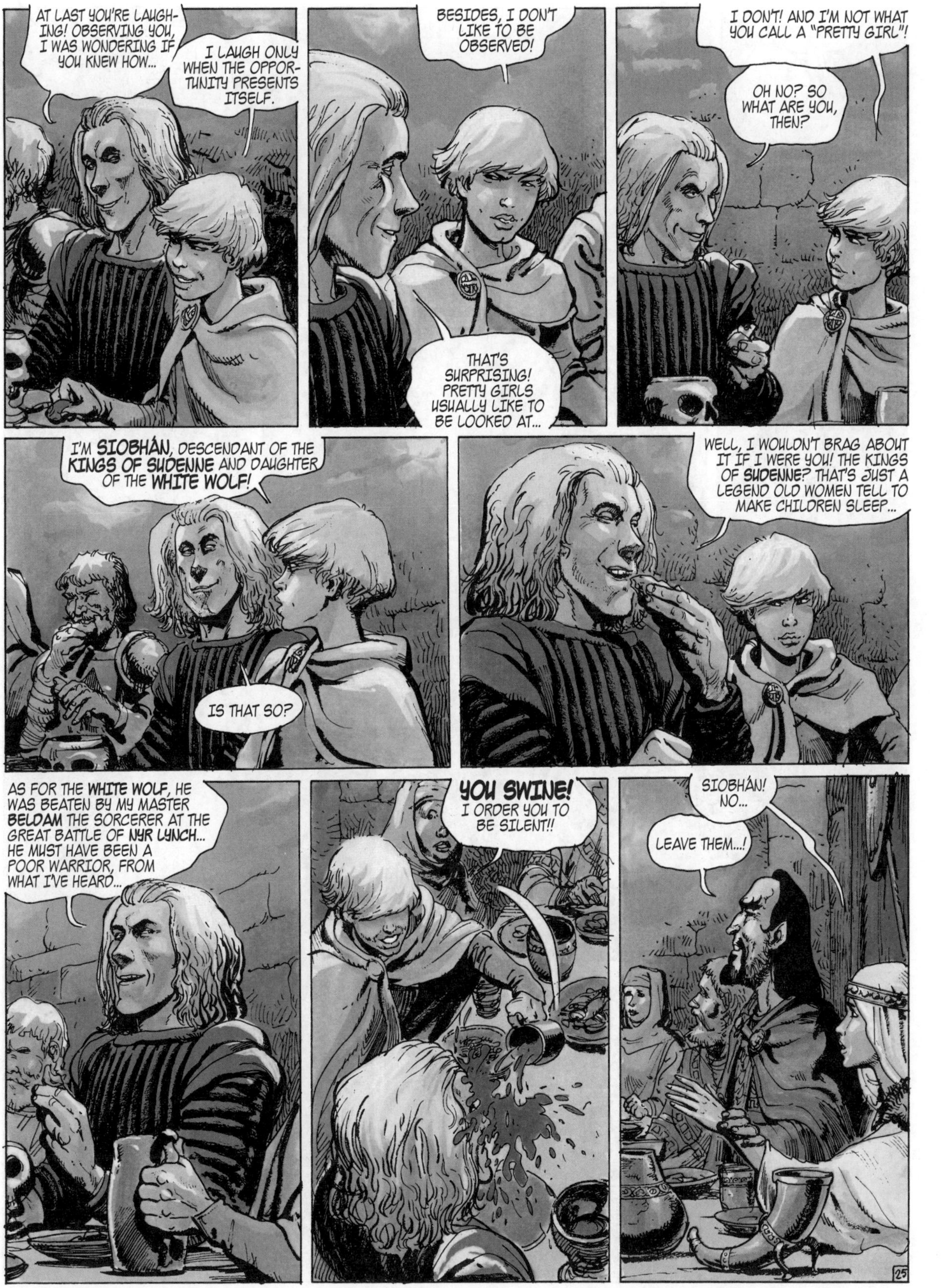
AT LAST YOU'RE LAUGHING! OBSERVING YOU, I WAS WONDERING IF YOU KNEW HOW...
I LAUGH ONLY WHEN THE OPPORTUNITY PRESENTS ITSELF.
BESIDES, I DON'T LIKE TO BE OBSERVED!
THAT'S SURPRISING! PRETTY GIRLS USUALLY LIKE TO BE LOOKED AT...
I DON'T! AND I'M NOT WHAT YOU CALL A "PRETTY GIRL"!
OH NO? SO WHAT ARE YOU, THEN?
I'M SIOBHÁN, DESCENDANT OF THE KINGS OF SUDENNE AND DAUGHTER OF THE WHITE WOLF!
IS THAT SO?
WELL, I WOULDN'T BRAG ABOUT IT IF I WERE YOU! THE KINGS OF SUDENNE? THAT'S JUST A LEGEND OLD WOMEN TELL TO MAKE CHILDREN SLEEP...
AS FOR THE WHITE WOLF, HE WAS BEATEN BY MY MASTER BELDAM THE SORCERER AT THE GREAT BATTLE OF NYR LYNCH... HE MUST HAVE BEEN A POOR WARRIOR, FROM WHAT I'VE HEARD...
YOU SWINE! I ORDER YOU TO BE SILENT!!
SIOBHÁN! NO...
LEAVE THEM...!
25

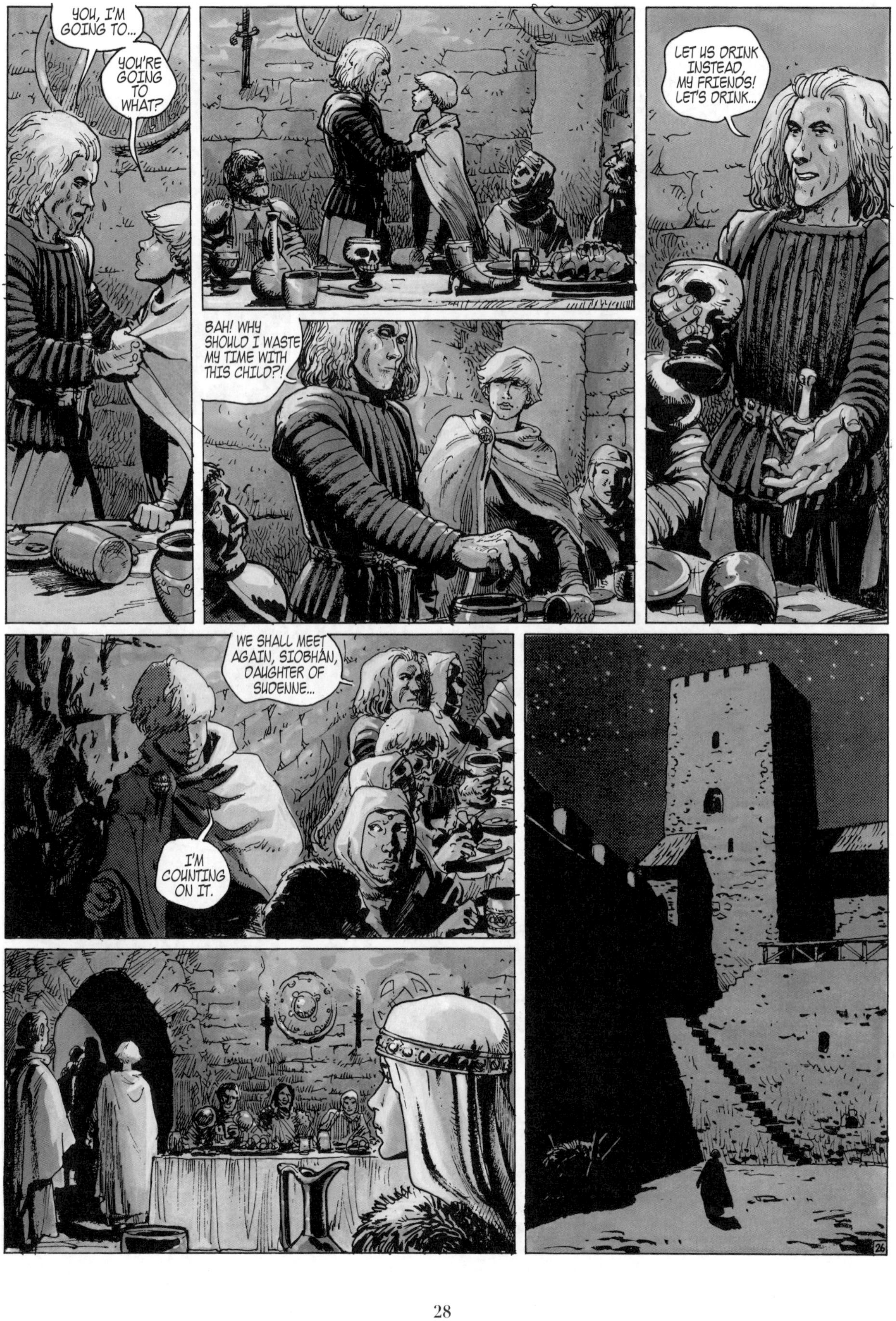
YOU, I'M GOING TO...
YOU'RE GOING TO WHAT?
LET US DRINK INSTEAD, MY FRIENDS! LET'S DRINK...
BAH! WHY SHOULD I WASTE MY TIME WITH THIS CHILD?!
WE SHALL MEET AGAIN, SIOBHAN, DAUGHTER OF SUDENNE...
I'M COUNTING ON IT.
26

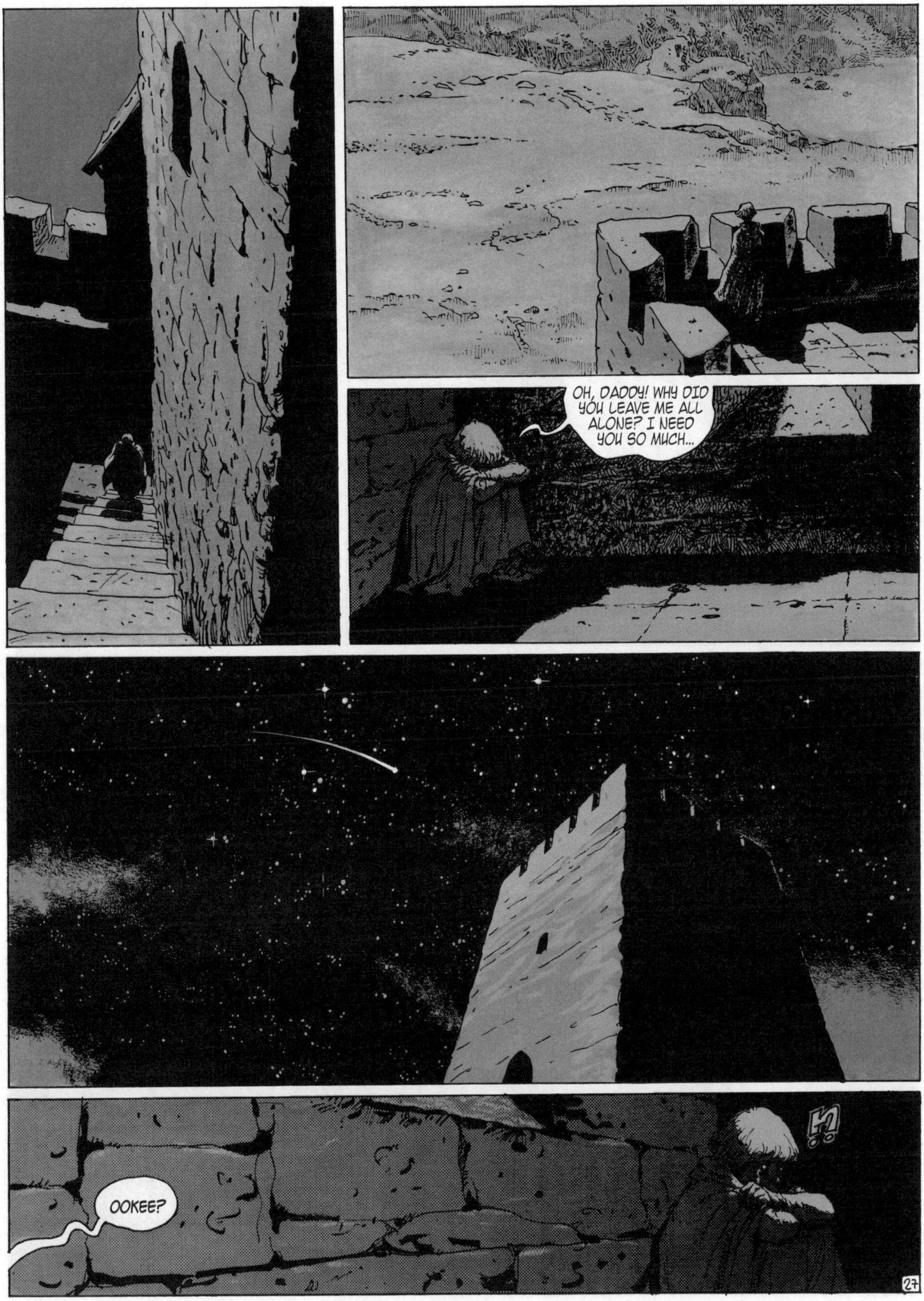
OH, DADDY! WHY DID YOU LEAVE ME ALL ALONE? I NEED YOU SO MUCH...
OOKEE?
27

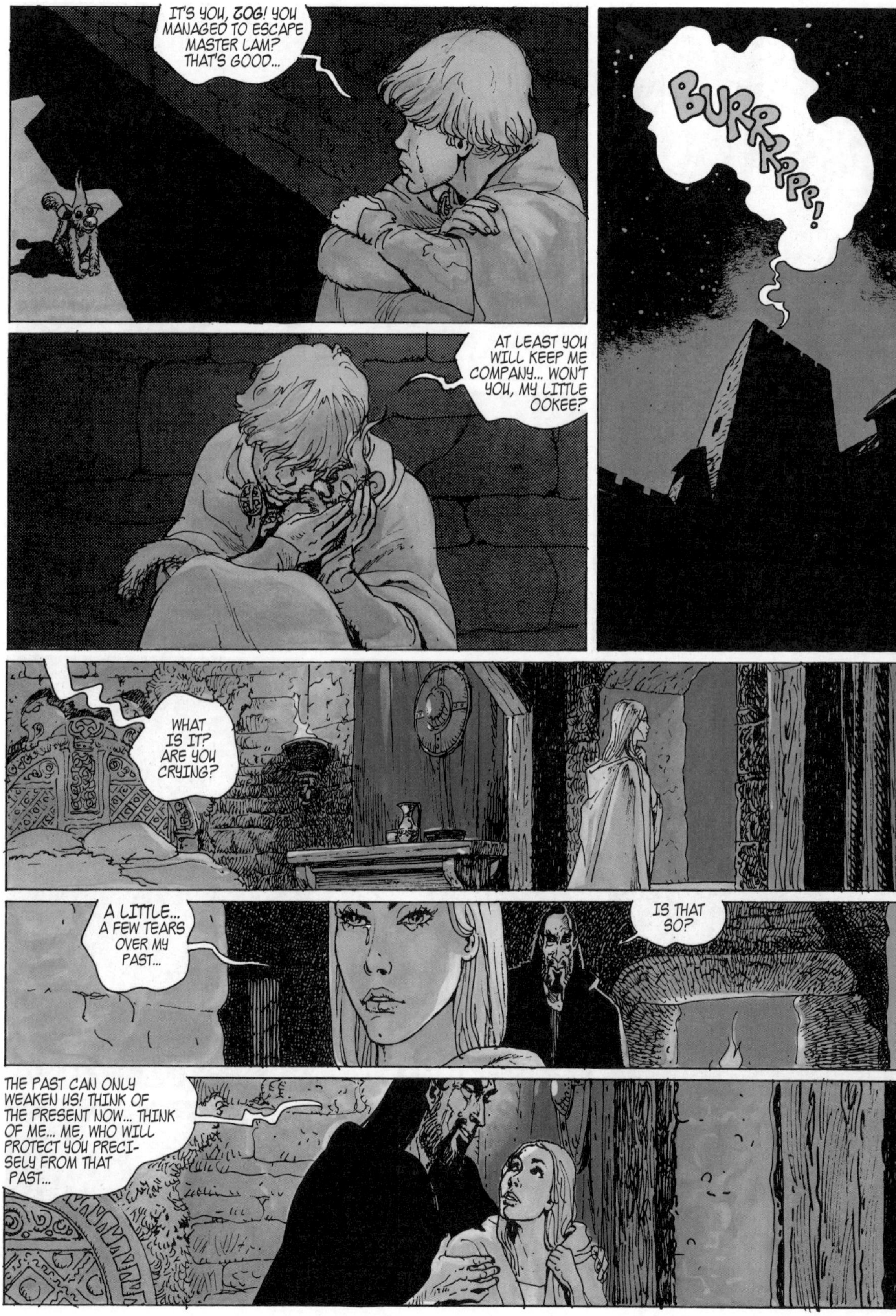
IT'S YOU, ZOG! YOU MANAGED TO ESCAPE MASTER LAM? THAT'S GOOD...
BURRRPPP!
AT LEAST YOU WILL KEEP ME COMPANY... WON'T YOU, MY LITTLE OOKEE?
WHAT IS IT? ARE YOU CRYING?
A LITTLE... A FEW TEARS OVER MY PAST...
IS THAT SO?
THE PAST CAN ONLY WEAKEN US! THINK OF THE PRESENT NOW... THINK OF ME... ME, WHO WILL PROTECT YOU PRECI-SELY FROM THAT PAST...
28

MY DAUGHTER... MY LITTLE SIOBHÁN... YOU WON'T FORGET ABOUT HER?

I WILL LOOK AFTER HER AS I PROMISED YOU...

AHHH

NO... I... PLEASE... NOT THIS... NOT THIS...

SILENCE! YOU WILL FORGET WHAT YOU SEE, FOR SOME MYSTERIES BELONG TO ME ALONE!

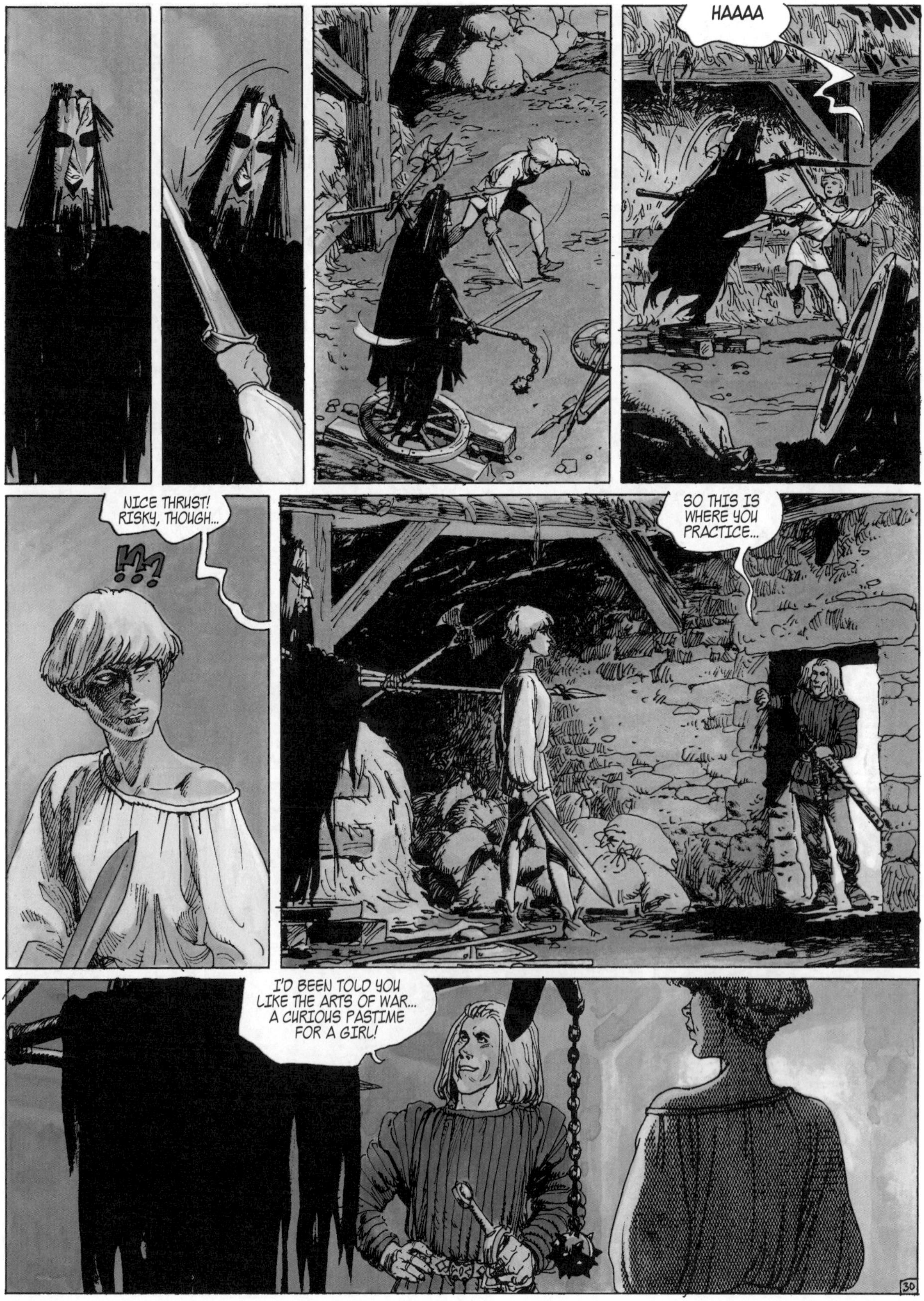
HAAAA
NICE THRUST! RISKY, THOUGH...
!??
SO THIS IS WHERE YOU PRACTICE...
I'D BEEN TOLD YOU LIKE THE ARTS OF WAR... A CURIOUS PASTIME FOR A GIRL!
30

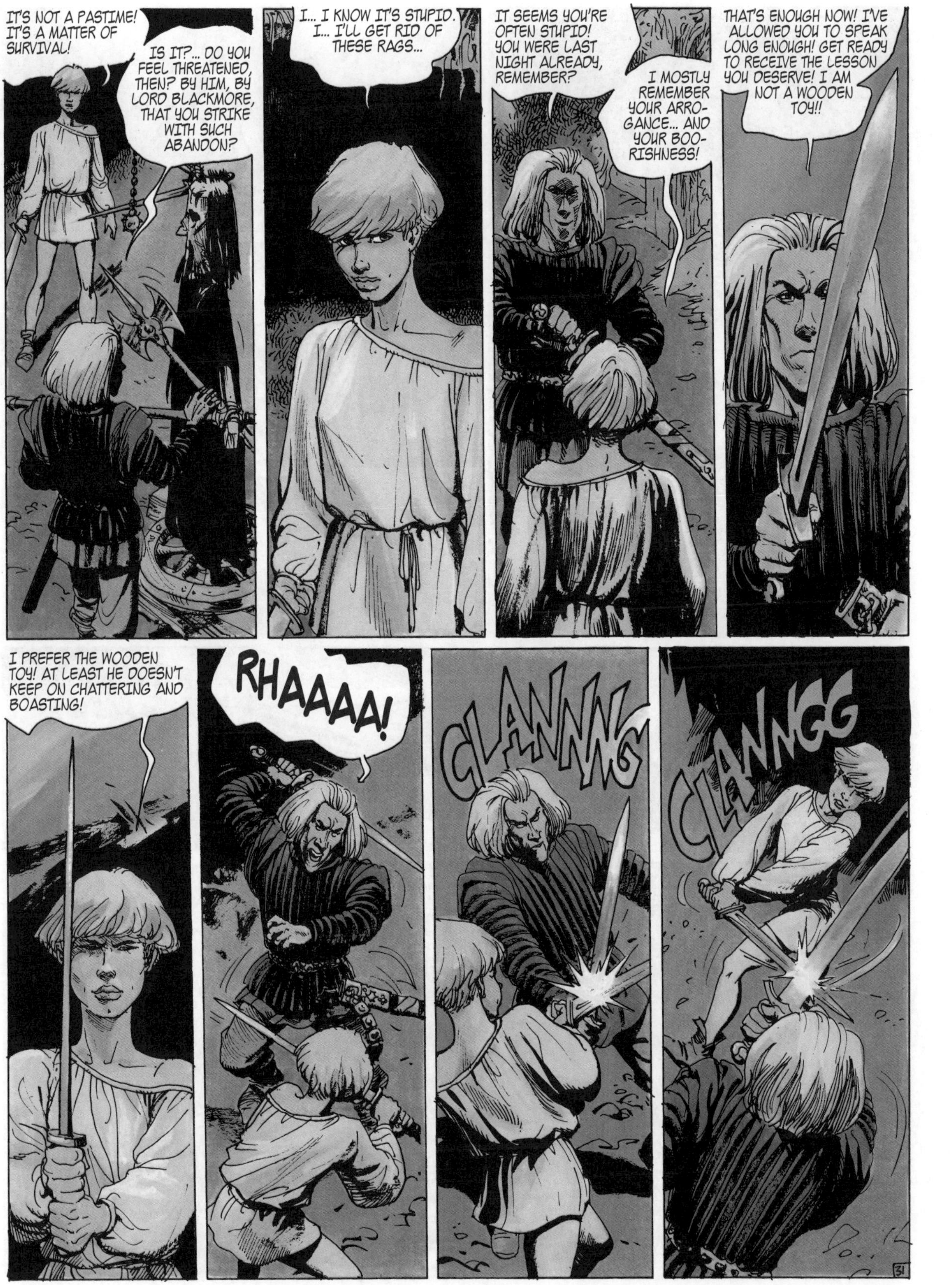
IT'S NOT A PASTIME! IT'S A MATTER OF SURVIVAL!
IS IT?... DO YOU FEEL THREATENED, THEN? BY HIM, BY LORD BLACKMORE, THAT YOU STRIKE WITH SUCH ABANDON?
I... I KNOW IT'S STUPID. I... I'LL GET RID OF THESE RAGS...
IT SEEMS YOU'RE OFTEN STUPID! YOU WERE LAST NIGHT ALREADY, REMEMBER?
I MOSTLY REMEMBER YOUR ARRO-GANCE... AND YOUR BOO-RISHNESS!
THAT'S ENOUGH NOW! I'VE ALLOWED YOU TO SPEAK LONG ENOUGH! GET READY TO RECEIVE THE LESSON YOU DESERVE! I AM NOT A WOODEN TOY!!
I PREFER THE WOODEN TOY! AT LEAST HE DOESN'T KEEP ON CHATTERING AND BOASTING!
RHAAAAA!
CLANNNG
CLANNGG
31

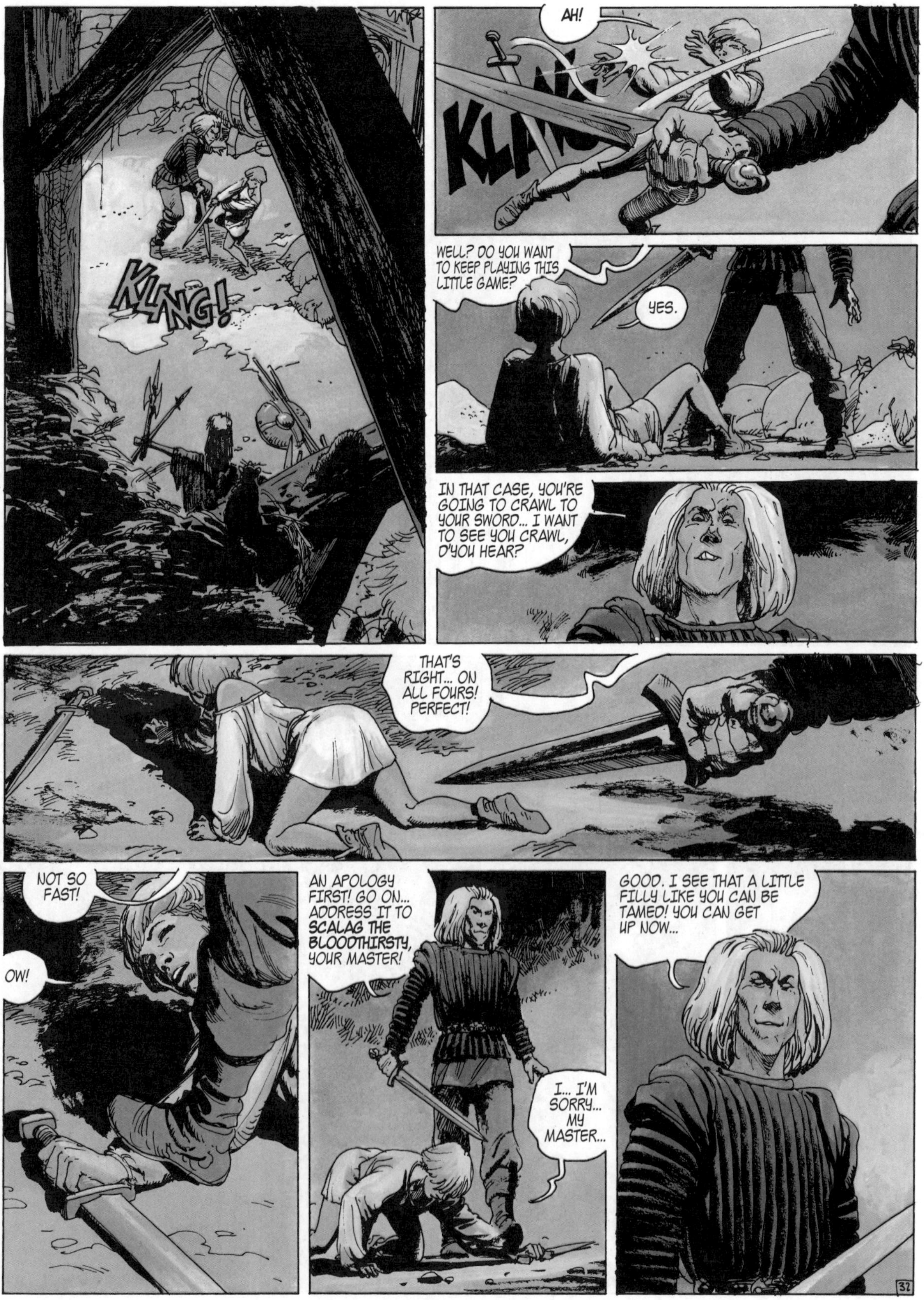
KLING!
AH!
KLANG
WELL? DO YOU WANT TO KEEP PLAYING THIS LITTLE GAME?
YES.
IN THAT CASE, YOU'RE GOING TO CRAWL TO YOUR SWORD... I WANT TO SEE YOU CRAWL, D'YOU HEAR?
THAT'S RIGHT... ON ALL FOURS! PERFECT!
NOT SO FAST!
OW!
AN APOLOGY FIRST! GO ON... ADDRESS IT TO **SCALAG THE BLOODTHIRSTY**, YOUR MASTER!
I... I'M SORRY... MY MASTER...
GOOD. I SEE THAT A LITTLE FILLY LIKE YOU CAN BE TAMED! YOU CAN GET UP NOW...
32

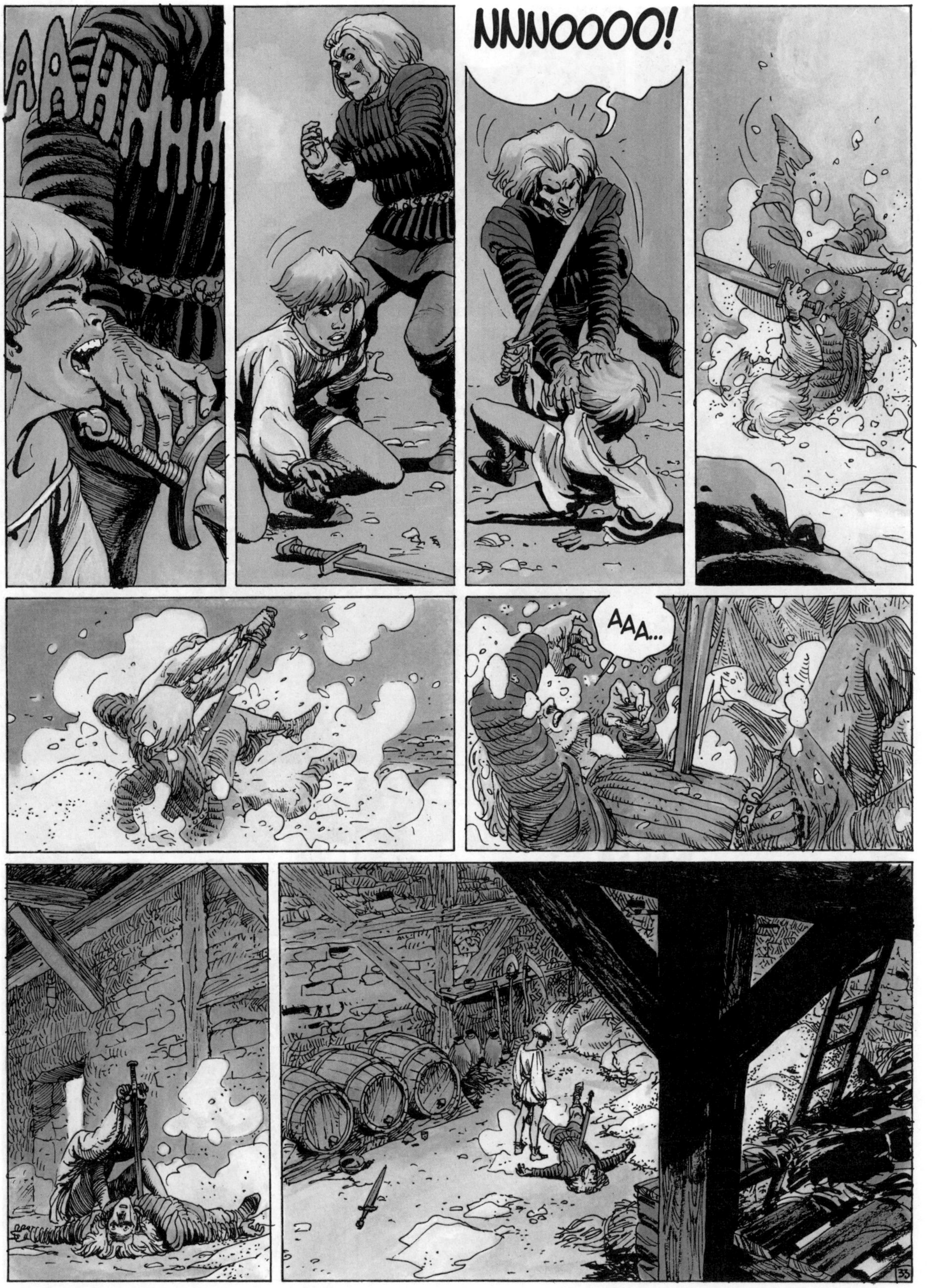
AAHHHHH
NNNOOOO!
AAA...
33

MY LORD! COME AND SEE!!!

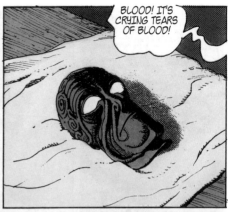

BLOOD! IT'S CRYING TEARS OF BLOOD!

IT'S GOING TO SPEAK...

THE SON OF **AEGIR**, GOD OF WRATH, SPEAKS THROUGH ME. HE CRIES TEARS OF BLOOD, FOR HE HAS LOST ONE OF HIS OWN... HIS GRIEF IS IMMENSE...

...AND IT ACCUSES YOU, FOR YOU COULD NOT FORESEE! HAS YOUR POWER BECOME SO BLIND THAT YOU LET THE SONG OF REBELLION PASS BEFORE YOU?

WILL YOU LET IT WHISPER WORDS OF COMFORT AND REVENGE INTO THE SKULL OF THE **WHITE WOLF**?!?... THE SON OF AEGIR MUST KNOW... HE AWAITS.

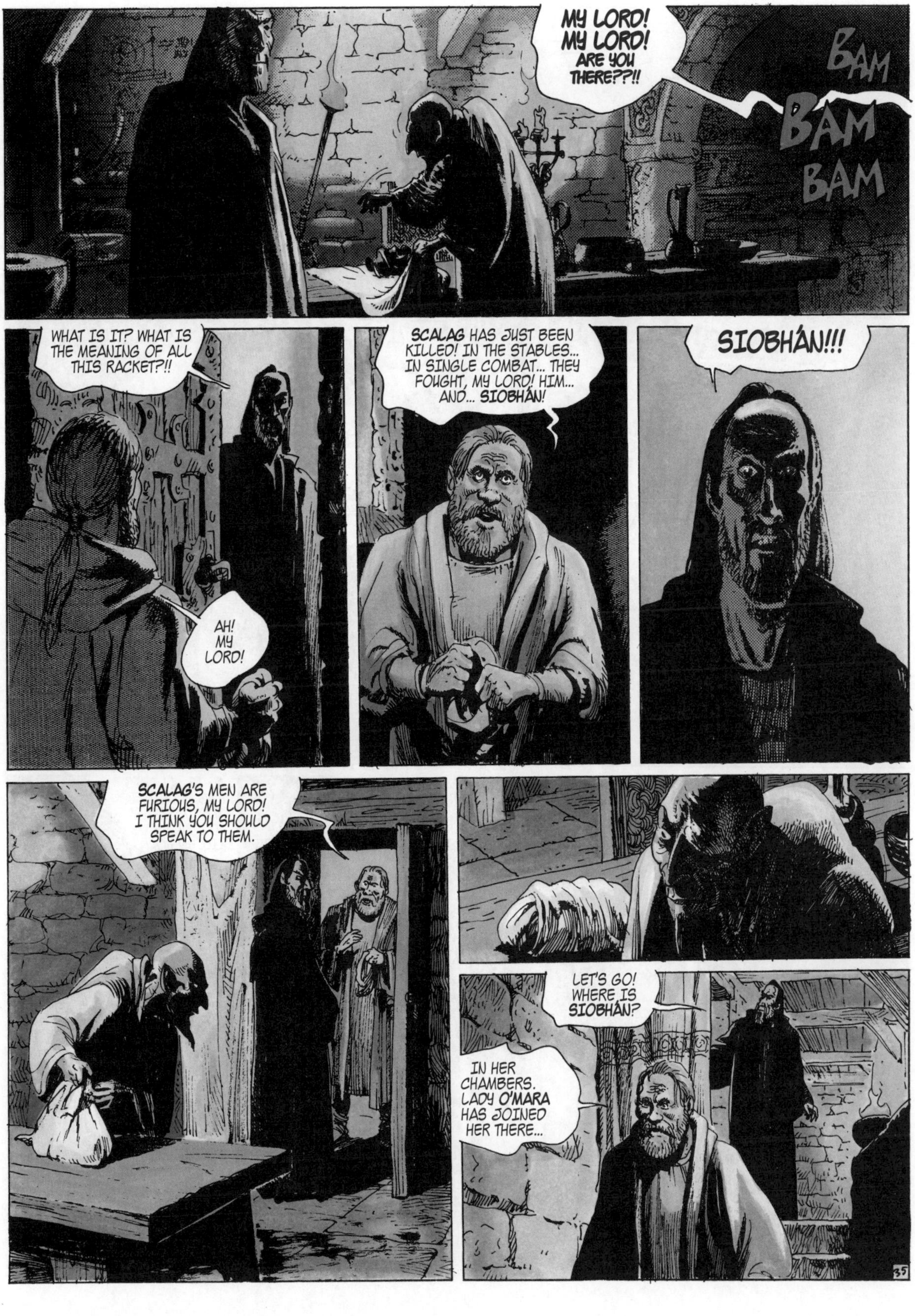
MY LORD!
MY LORD!
ARE YOU THERE??!!
BAM
BAM
BAM
WHAT IS IT? WHAT IS THE MEANING OF ALL THIS RACKET?!!
AH! MY LORD!
SCALAG HAS JUST BEEN KILLED! IN THE STABLES... IN SINGLE COMBAT... THEY FOUGHT, MY LORD! HIM... AND... SIOBHÁN!
SIOBHÁN!!!
SCALAG'S MEN ARE FURIOUS, MY LORD! I THINK YOU SHOULD SPEAK TO THEM.
LET'S GO! WHERE IS SIOBHÁN?
IN HER CHAMBERS. LADY O'MARA HAS JOINED HER THERE...
35

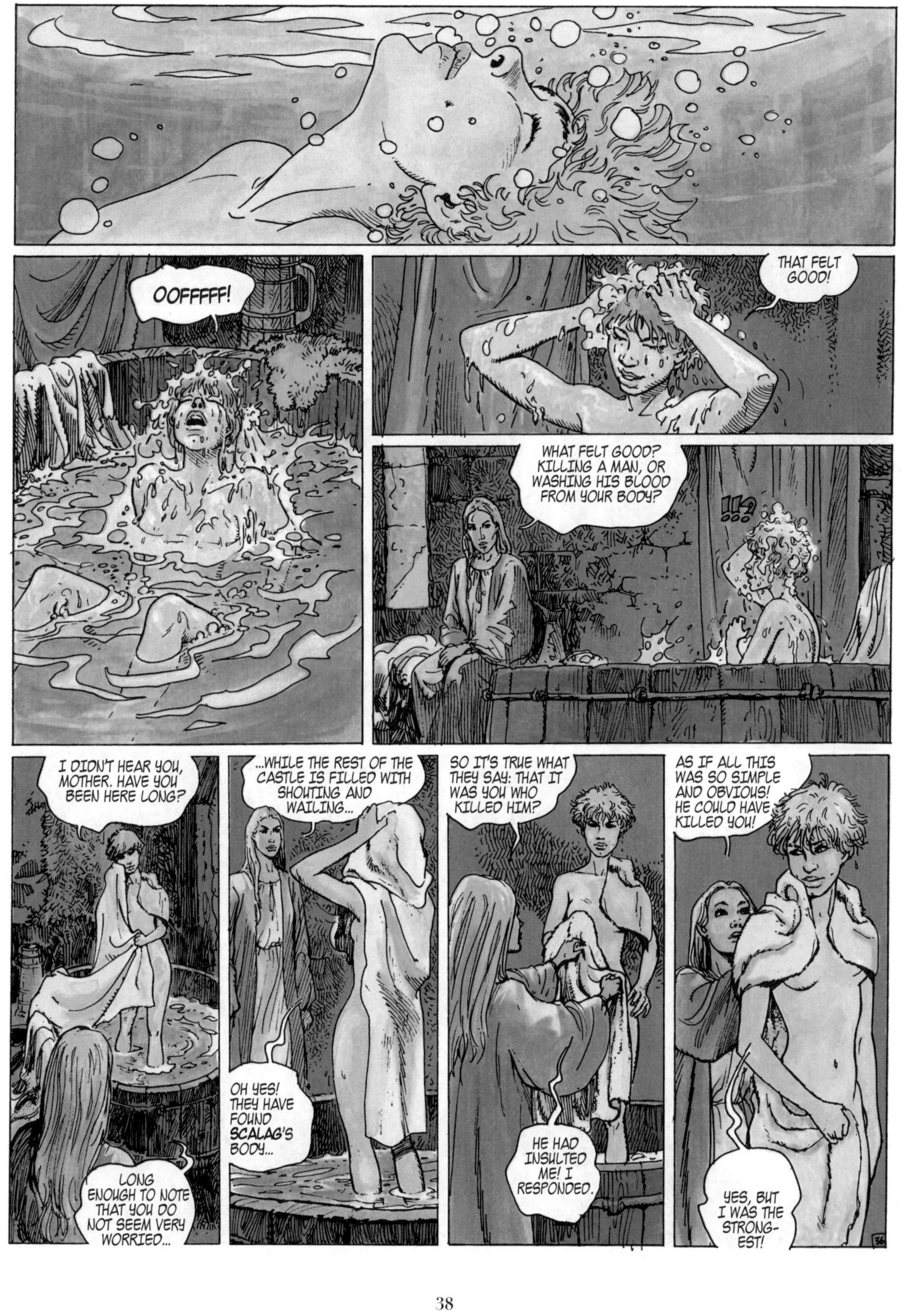
OOFFFFF!
THAT FELT GOOD!
WHAT FELT GOOD? KILLING A MAN, OR WASHING HIS BLOOD FROM YOUR BODY?
I DIDN'T HEAR YOU, MOTHER. HAVE YOU BEEN HERE LONG?
LONG ENOUGH TO NOTE THAT YOU DO NOT SEEM VERY WORRIED...
...WHILE THE REST OF THE CASTLE IS FILLED WITH SHOUTING AND WAILING...
OH YES! THEY HAVE FOUND SCALAG'S BODY...
SO IT'S TRUE WHAT THEY SAY: THAT IT WAS YOU WHO KILLED HIM?
HE HAD INSULTED ME! I RESPONDED.
AS IF ALL THIS WAS SO SIMPLE AND OBVIOUS! HE COULD HAVE KILLED YOU!
YES, BUT I WAS THE STRONG-EST!

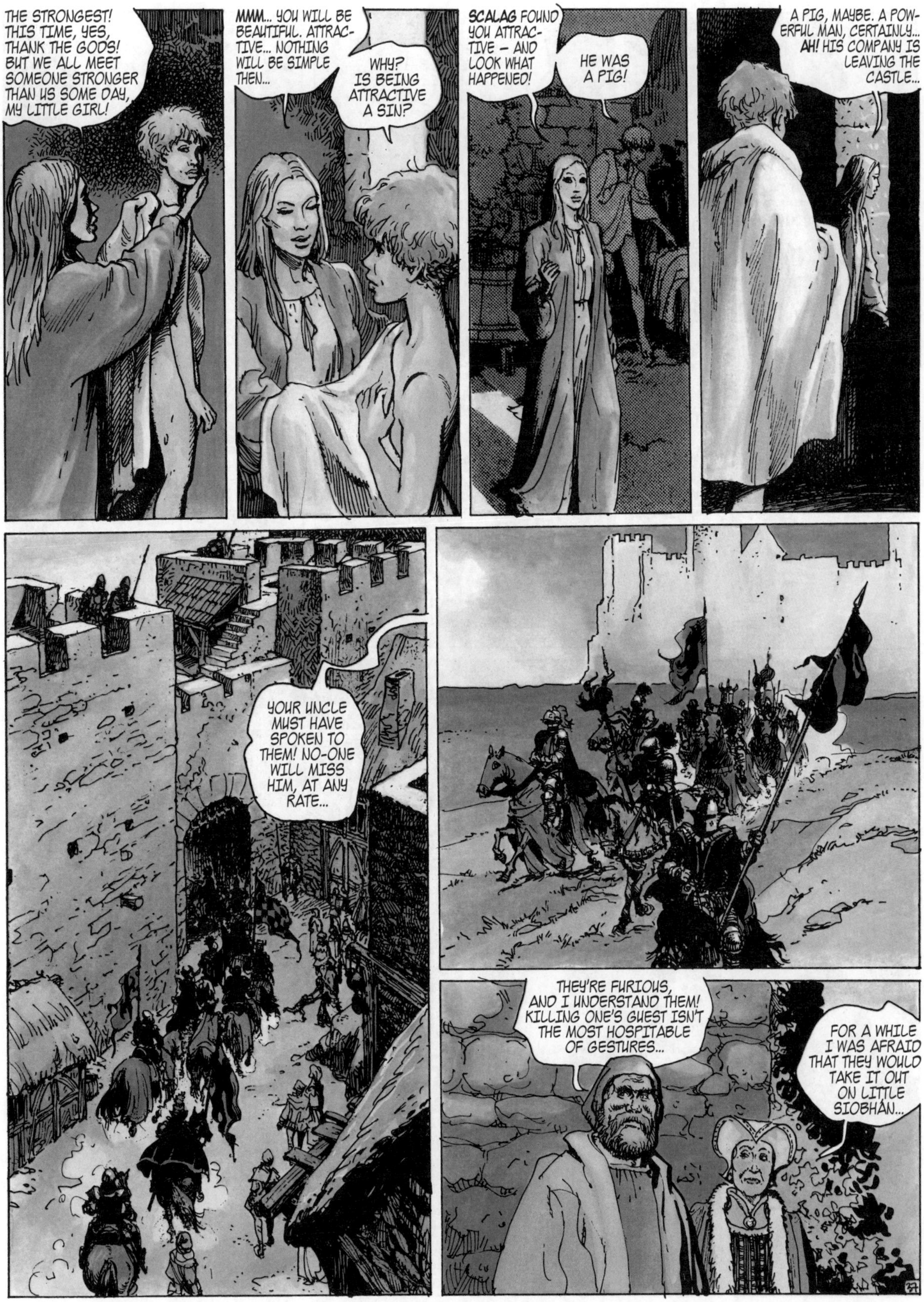
THE STRONGEST! THIS TIME, YES, THANK THE GODS! BUT WE ALL MEET SOMEONE STRONGER THAN US SOME DAY, MY LITTLE GIRL!
MMM... YOU WILL BE BEAUTIFUL. ATTRACTIVE... NOTHING WILL BE SIMPLE THEN...
WHY? IS BEING ATTRACTIVE A SIN?
SCALAG FOUND YOU ATTRACTIVE – AND LOOK WHAT HAPPENED!
HE WAS A PIG!
A PIG, MAYBE. A POWERFUL MAN, CERTAINLY... AH! HIS COMPANY IS LEAVING THE CASTLE...
YOUR UNCLE MUST HAVE SPOKEN TO THEM! NO-ONE WILL MISS HIM, AT ANY RATE...
THEY'RE FURIOUS, AND I UNDERSTAND THEM! KILLING ONE'S GUEST ISN'T THE MOST HOSPITABLE OF GESTURES...
FOR A WHILE I WAS AFRAID THAT THEY WOULD TAKE IT OUT ON LITTLE SIOBHAN...

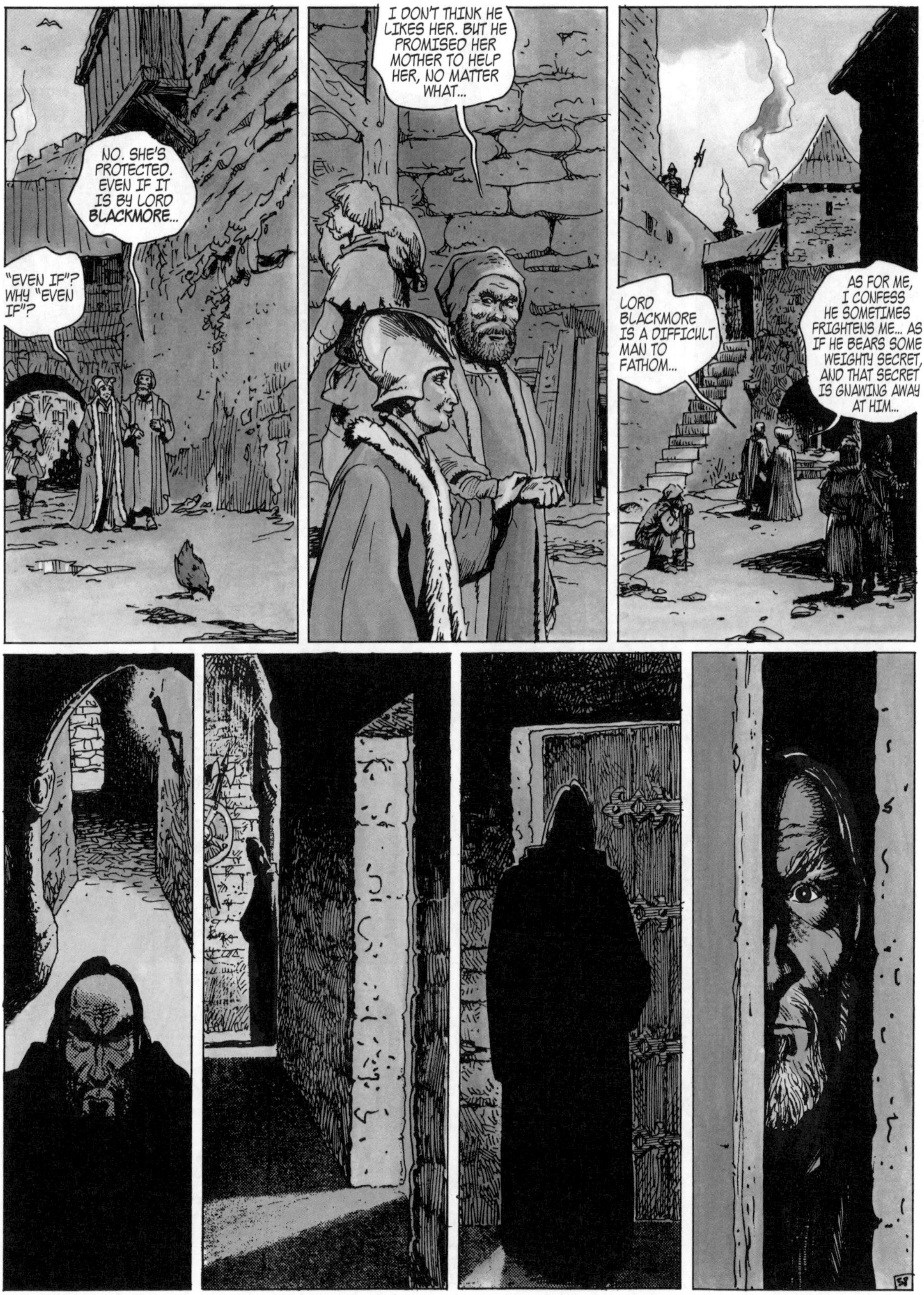
NO. SHE'S PROTECTED. EVEN IF IT IS BY LORD BLACKMORE...
"EVEN IF"? WHY "EVEN IF"?
I DON'T THINK HE LIKES HER. BUT HE PROMISED HER MOTHER TO HELP HER, NO MATTER WHAT...
LORD BLACKMORE IS A DIFFICULT MAN TO FATHOM...
AS FOR ME, I CONFESS HE SOMETIMES FRIGHTENS ME... AS IF HE BEARS SOME WEIGHTY SECRET, AND THAT SECRET IS GNAWING AWAY AT HIM...
58

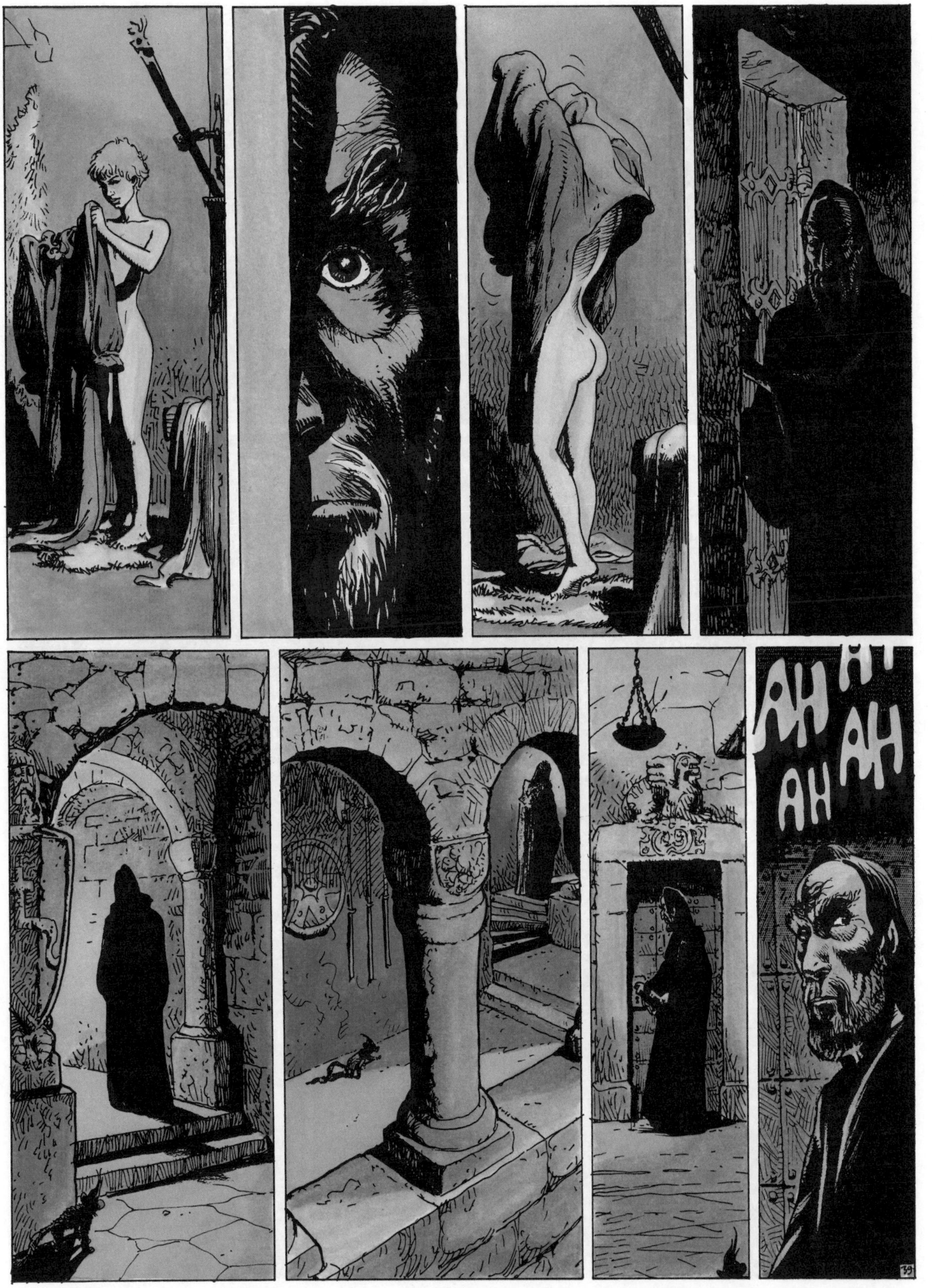
AH
AH
AH
39

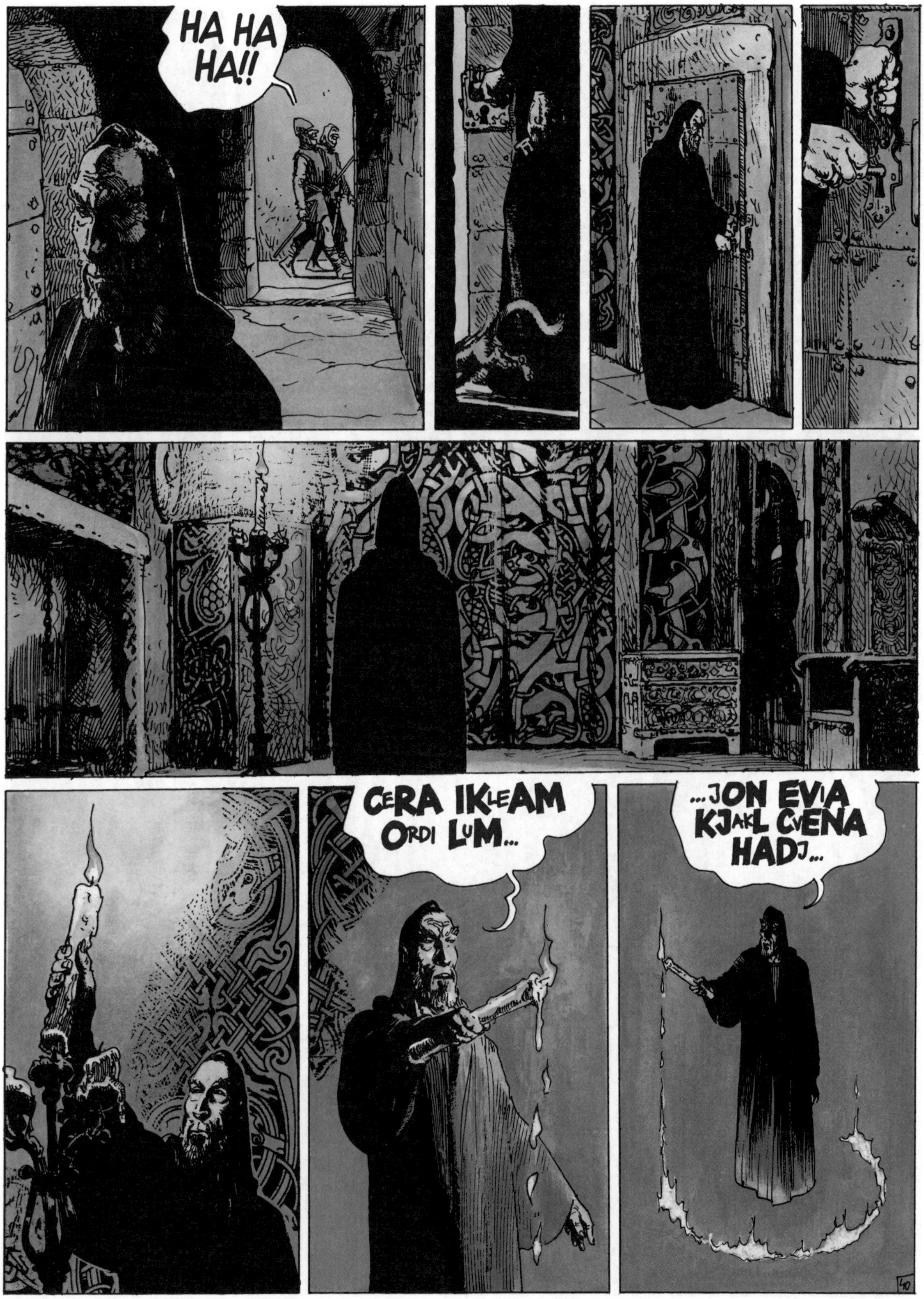
HA HA HA!!
CERA IKLEAM ORDI LUM...
...JON EVIA KJAKL CVENA HADJ...
40

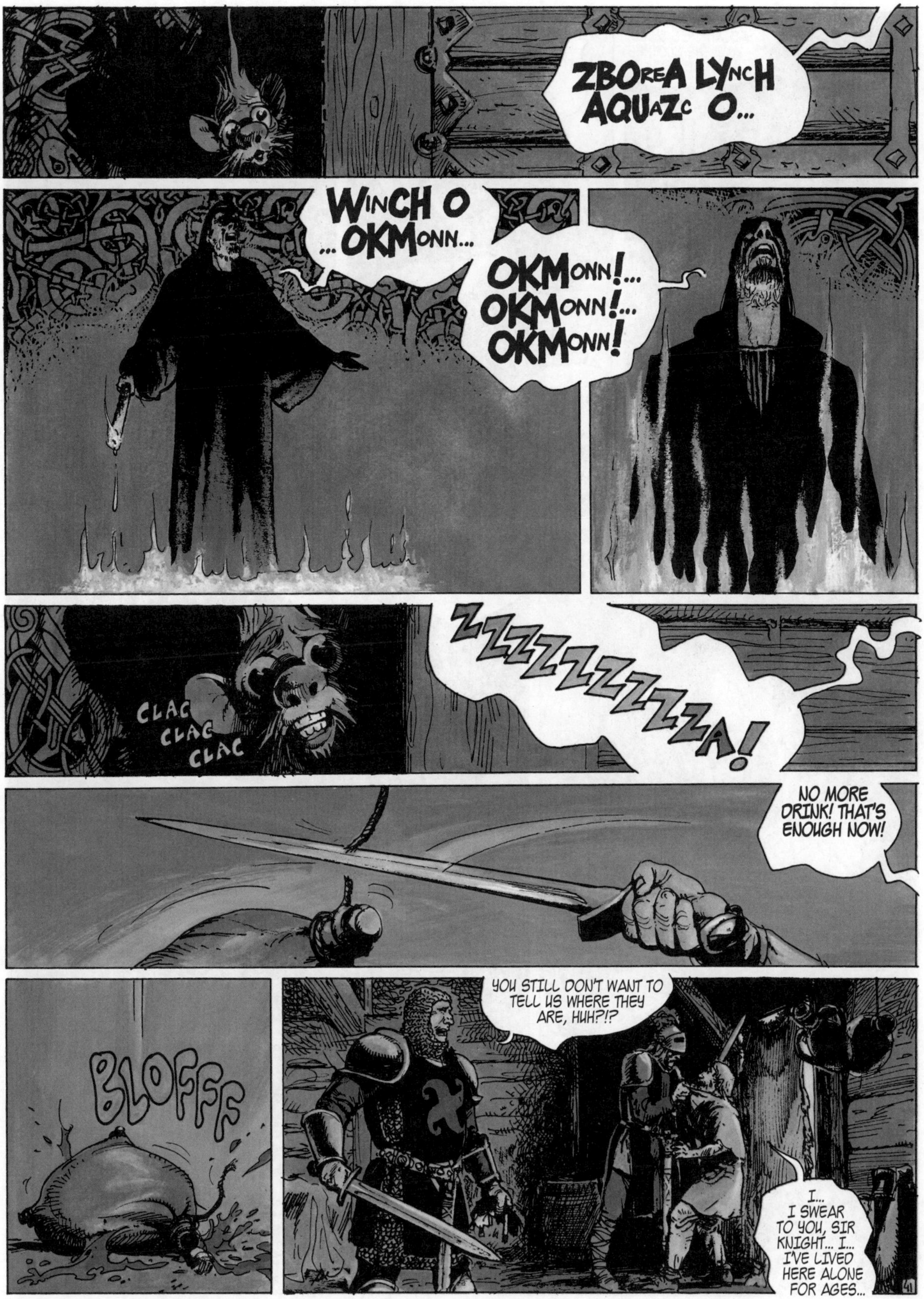

ZBOREA LYNCH AQUAZC O...
WINCH O ...OKMONN...
OKMONN!... OKMONN!... OKMONN!
CLAC CLAC CLAC
ZZZZZZZZZZZA!
NO MORE DRINK! THAT'S ENOUGH NOW!
BLOFFF
YOU STILL DON'T WANT TO TELL US WHERE THEY ARE, HUH?!?
I... I SWEAR TO YOU, SIR KNIGHT... I... I'VE LIVED HERE ALONE FOR AGES...
41

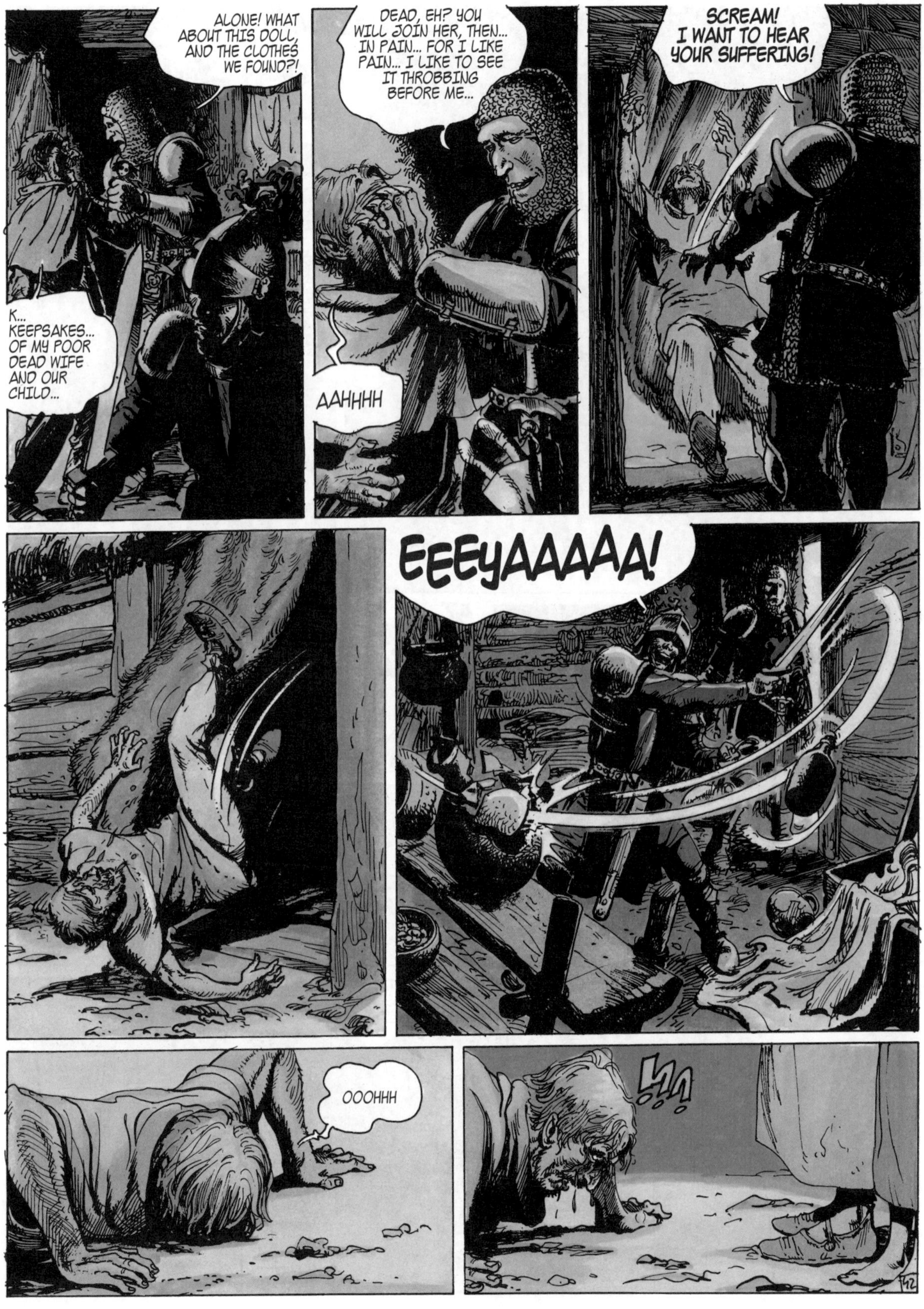

ALONE! WHAT ABOUT THIS DOLL, AND THE CLOTHES WE FOUND?!
K... KEEPSAKES... OF MY POOR DEAD WIFE AND OUR CHILD...
DEAD, EH? YOU WILL JOIN HER, THEN... IN PAIN... FOR I LIKE PAIN... I LIKE TO SEE IT THROBBING BEFORE ME...
AAHHHH
SCREAM! I WANT TO HEAR YOUR SUFFERING!
EEEYAAAAAA!
OOOHHH
!?!?

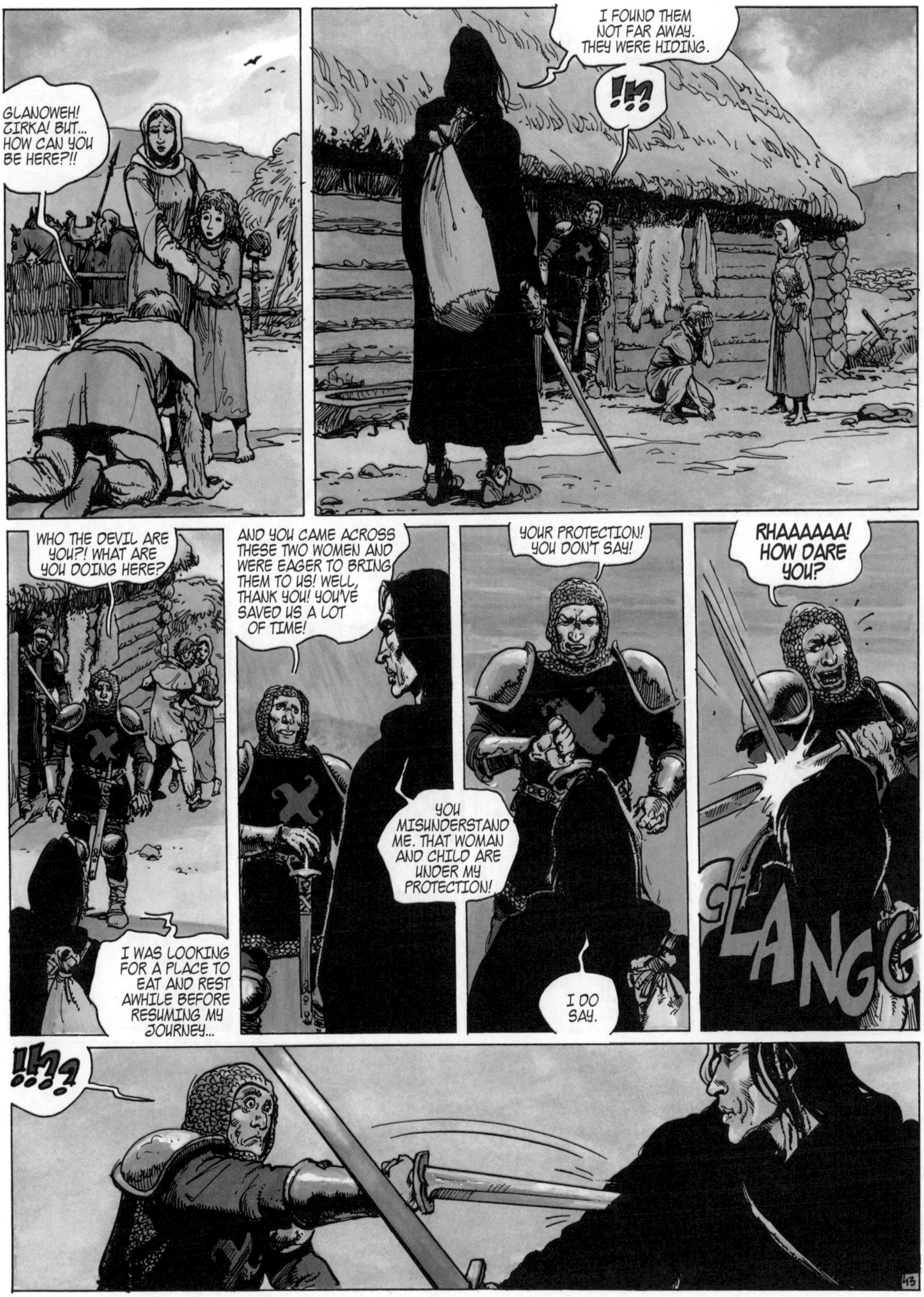
GLANOWEH! ZIRKA! BUT... HOW CAN YOU BE HERE?!!
I FOUND THEM NOT FAR AWAY. THEY WERE HIDING.
!!??
WHO THE DEVIL ARE YOU?! WHAT ARE YOU DOING HERE?
I WAS LOOKING FOR A PLACE TO EAT AND REST AWHILE BEFORE RESUMING MY JOURNEY...
AND YOU CAME ACROSS THESE TWO WOMEN AND WERE EAGER TO BRING THEM TO US! WELL, THANK YOU! YOU'VE SAVED US A LOT OF TIME!
YOU MISUNDERSTAND ME. THAT WOMAN AND CHILD ARE UNDER MY PROTECTION!
YOUR PROTECTION! YOU DON'T SAY!
I DO SAY.
RHAAAAAA! HOW DARE YOU?
CLANGG
!!???
43

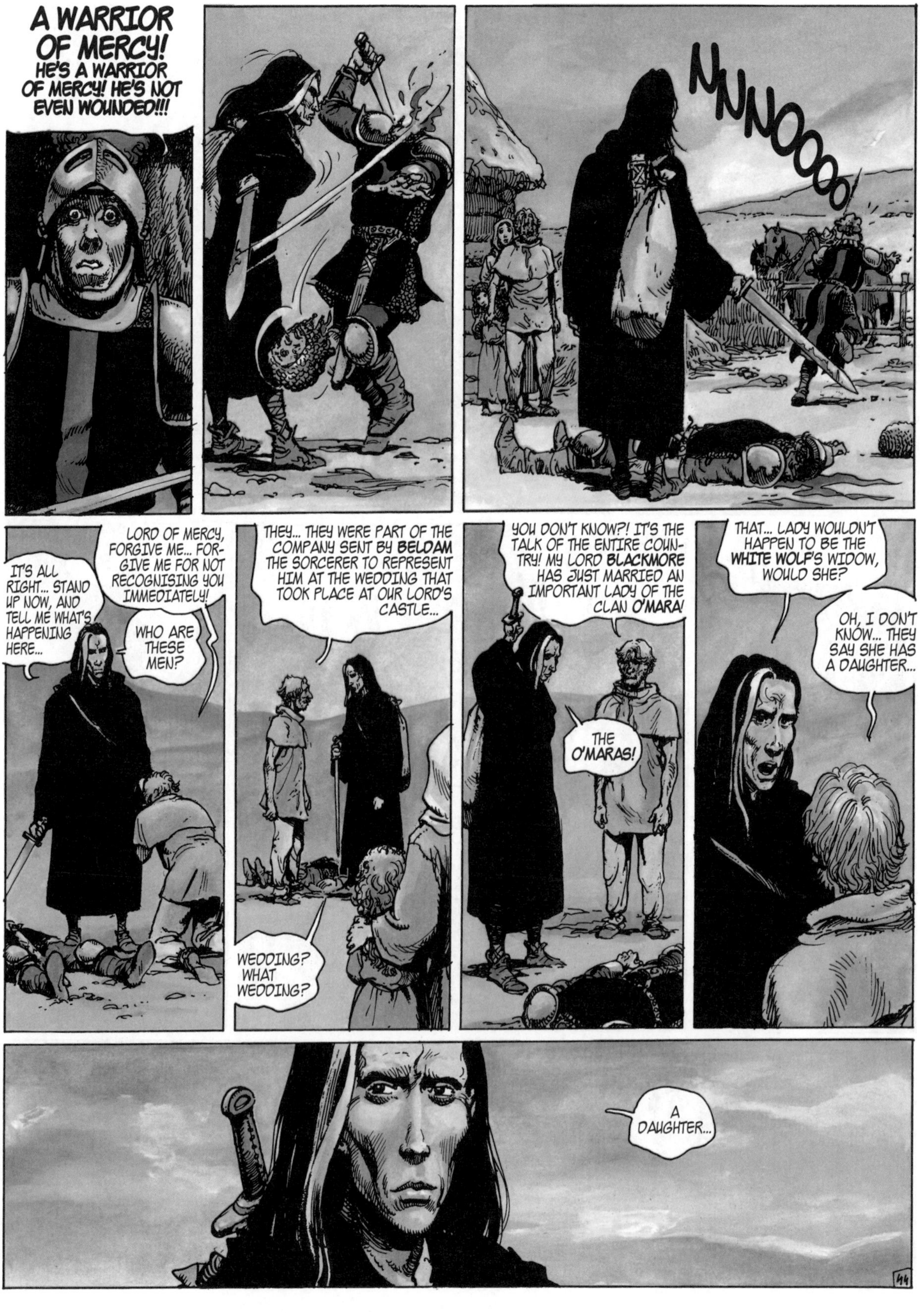
A WARRIOR OF MERCY!
HE'S A WARRIOR OF MERCY! HE'S NOT EVEN WOUNDED!!!
NNNOOOO
IT'S ALL RIGHT... STAND UP NOW, AND TELL ME WHAT'S HAPPENING HERE...
LORD OF MERCY, FORGIVE ME... FORGIVE ME FOR NOT RECOGNISING YOU IMMEDIATELY!
WHO ARE THESE MEN?
THEY... THEY WERE PART OF THE COMPANY SENT BY BELDAM THE SORCERER TO REPRESENT HIM AT THE WEDDING THAT TOOK PLACE AT OUR LORD'S CASTLE...
WEDDING? WHAT WEDDING?
YOU DON'T KNOW?! IT'S THE TALK OF THE ENTIRE COUNTRY! MY LORD BLACKMORE HAS JUST MARRIED AN IMPORTANT LADY OF THE CLAN O'MARA!
THE O'MARAS!
THAT... LADY WOULDN'T HAPPEN TO BE THE WHITE WOLF'S WIDOW, WOULD SHE?
OH, I DON'T KNOW... THEY SAY SHE HAS A DAUGHTER...
A DAUGHTER...
44

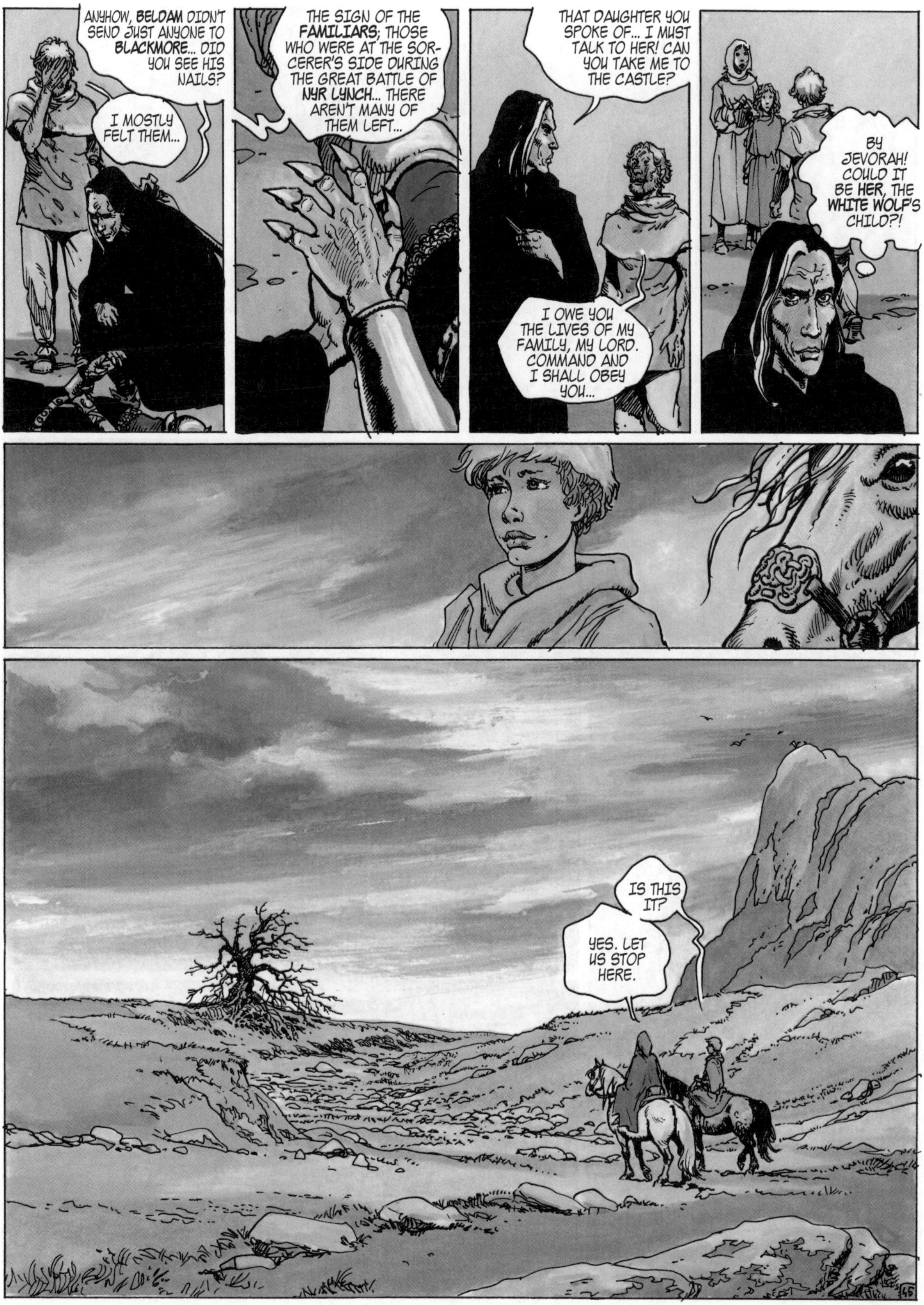
ANYHOW, BELDAM DIDN'T SEND JUST ANYONE TO BLACKMORE... DID YOU SEE HIS NAILS?
I MOSTLY FELT THEM...
THE SIGN OF THE FAMILIARS; THOSE WHO WERE AT THE SORCERER'S SIDE DURING THE GREAT BATTLE OF NYR LYNCH... THERE AREN'T MANY OF THEM LEFT...
THAT DAUGHTER YOU SPOKE OF... I MUST TALK TO HER! CAN YOU TAKE ME TO THE CASTLE?
I OWE YOU THE LIVES OF MY FAMILY, MY LORD. COMMAND AND I SHALL OBEY YOU...
BY JEVORAH! COULD IT BE HER, THE WHITE WOLF'S CHILD?!
IS THIS IT?
YES. LET US STOP HERE.
45

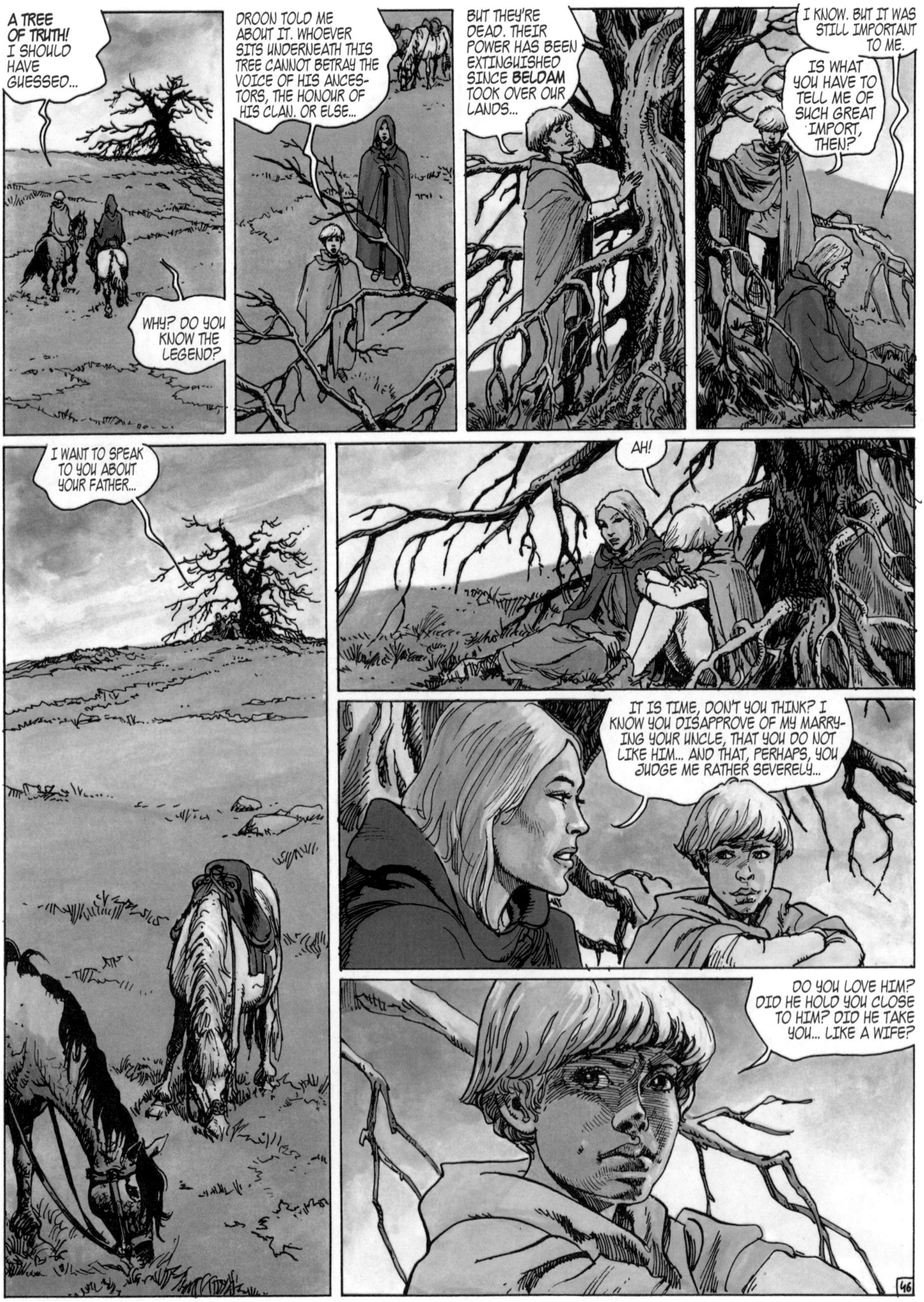
A TREE OF TRUTH! I SHOULD HAVE GUESSED...
WHY? DO YOU KNOW THE LEGEND?
DROON TOLD ME ABOUT IT. WHOEVER SITS UNDERNEATH THIS TREE CANNOT BETRAY THE VOICE OF HIS ANCES-TORS, THE HONOUR OF HIS CLAN. OR ELSE...
BUT THEY'RE DEAD. THEIR POWER HAS BEEN EXTINGUISHED SINCE BELDAM TOOK OVER OUR LANDS...
I KNOW. BUT IT WAS STILL IMPORTANT TO ME.
IS WHAT YOU HAVE TO TELL ME OF SUCH GREAT IMPORT, THEN?
I WANT TO SPEAK TO YOU ABOUT YOUR FATHER...
AH!
IT IS TIME, DON'T YOU THINK? I KNOW YOU DISAPPROVE OF MY MARRY-ING YOUR UNCLE, THAT YOU DO NOT LIKE HIM... AND THAT, PERHAPS, YOU JUDGE ME RATHER SEVERELY...
DO YOU LOVE HIM? DID HE HOLD YOU CLOSE TO HIM? DID HE TAKE YOU... LIKE A WIFE?
46

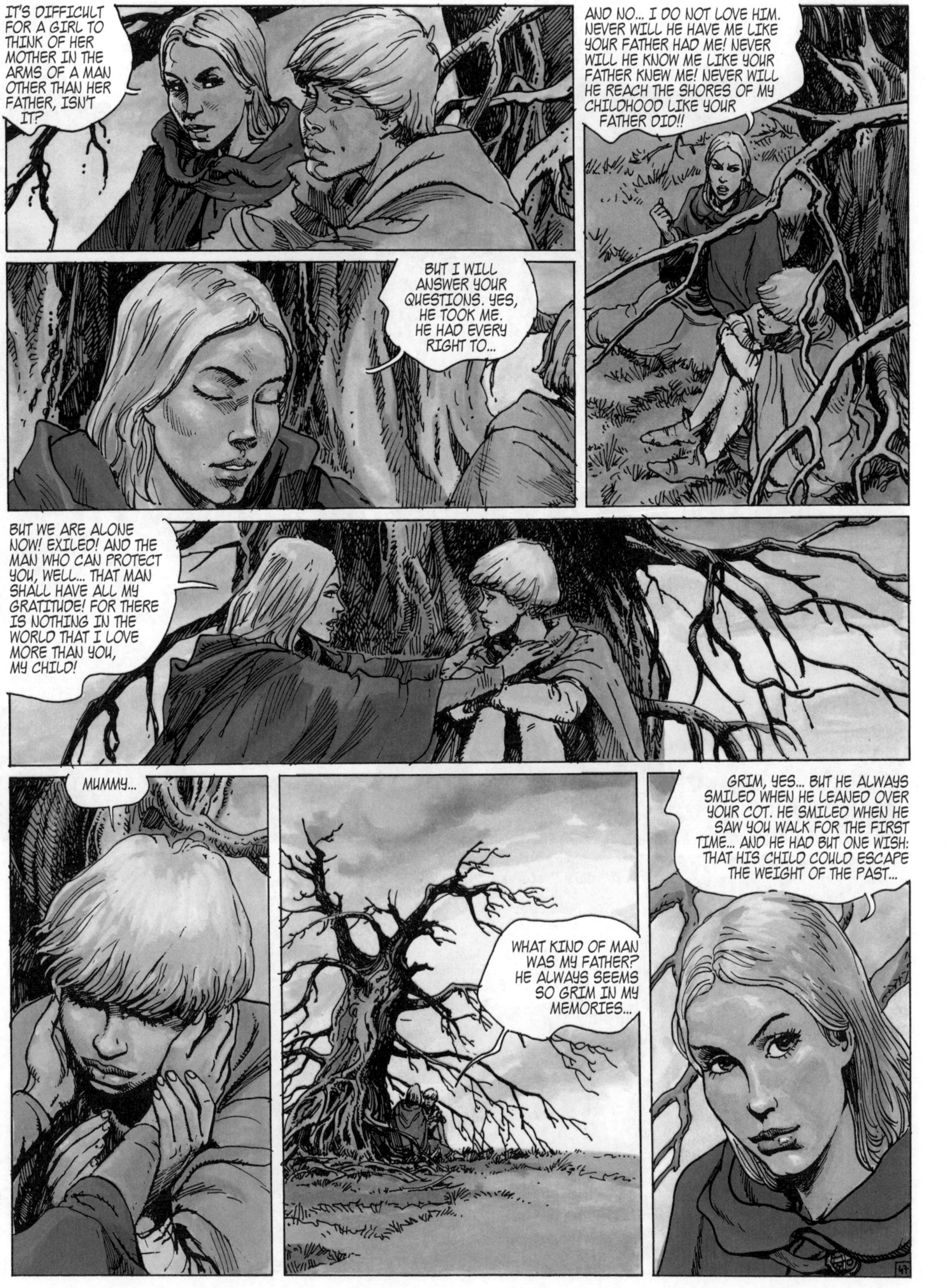
IT'S DIFFICULT FOR A GIRL TO THINK OF HER MOTHER IN THE ARMS OF A MAN OTHER THAN HER FATHER, ISN'T IT?
AND NO... I DO NOT LOVE HIM. NEVER WILL HE HAVE ME LIKE YOUR FATHER HAD ME! NEVER WILL HE KNOW ME LIKE YOUR FATHER KNEW ME! NEVER WILL HE REACH THE SHORES OF MY CHILDHOOD LIKE YOUR FATHER DID!!
BUT I WILL ANSWER YOUR QUESTIONS. YES, HE TOOK ME. HE HAD EVERY RIGHT TO...
BUT WE ARE ALONE NOW! EXILED! AND THE MAN WHO CAN PROTECT YOU, WELL... THAT MAN SHALL HAVE ALL MY GRATITUDE! FOR THERE IS NOTHING IN THE WORLD THAT I LOVE MORE THAN YOU, MY CHILD!
MUMMY...
WHAT KIND OF MAN WAS MY FATHER? HE ALWAYS SEEMS SO GRIM IN MY MEMORIES...
GRIM, YES... BUT HE ALWAYS SMILED WHEN HE LEANED OVER YOUR COT. HE SMILED WHEN HE SAW YOU WALK FOR THE FIRST TIME... AND HE HAD BUT ONE WISH: THAT HIS CHILD COULD ESCAPE THE WEIGHT OF THE PAST...
47

FROM TIME IMMEMORIAL, THE LAND OF **ERUIN DULEA** ALWAYS BELONGED TO THE KINGS OF **SUDENNE**. UNTIL THE DEATH OF **AVERUS**, YOUR GREAT-GRANDFATHER, WHO WAS SURVIVED ONLY BY A TEN-YEAR-OLD GIRL, LAETITIA...

NO MALE HEIRS! THAT GAVE FREE REIN TO GENERAL DISCORD, AS EACH CLAN RUSHED TO STAKE ITS CLAIM TO THE THRONE. BUT NONE WAS WORTHY OF IT.

THEN, FROM THE SCULLERY OF **AVERUS'S** CASTLE, THERE AROSE A GREAT CRY AND A HIDEOUS SHAPE APPEARED FROM BENEATH A RUBBISH-STREWN TABLE. A SCRAWNY, UGLY BOY, HIS BODY CRAWLING WITH VERMIN...

HE WOULD BECOME KNOWN TO ALL BY THE NAME OF **OBLA**...

...THE BASTARD OFFSPRING OF **AVERUS'S** DALLIANCE WITH A KITCHEN SLATTERN, A SCRAWNY WOMAN WITH LONG BLACK HAIR. PEOPLE SAID SHE WAS SOMETHING OF A WITCH, AND HAD CAST A SPELL ON THE KING... SOON AFTER THE CHILD WAS BORN, SHE WAS RUN OUT OF THE CASTLE, NEVER TO BE SEEN AGAIN...

48

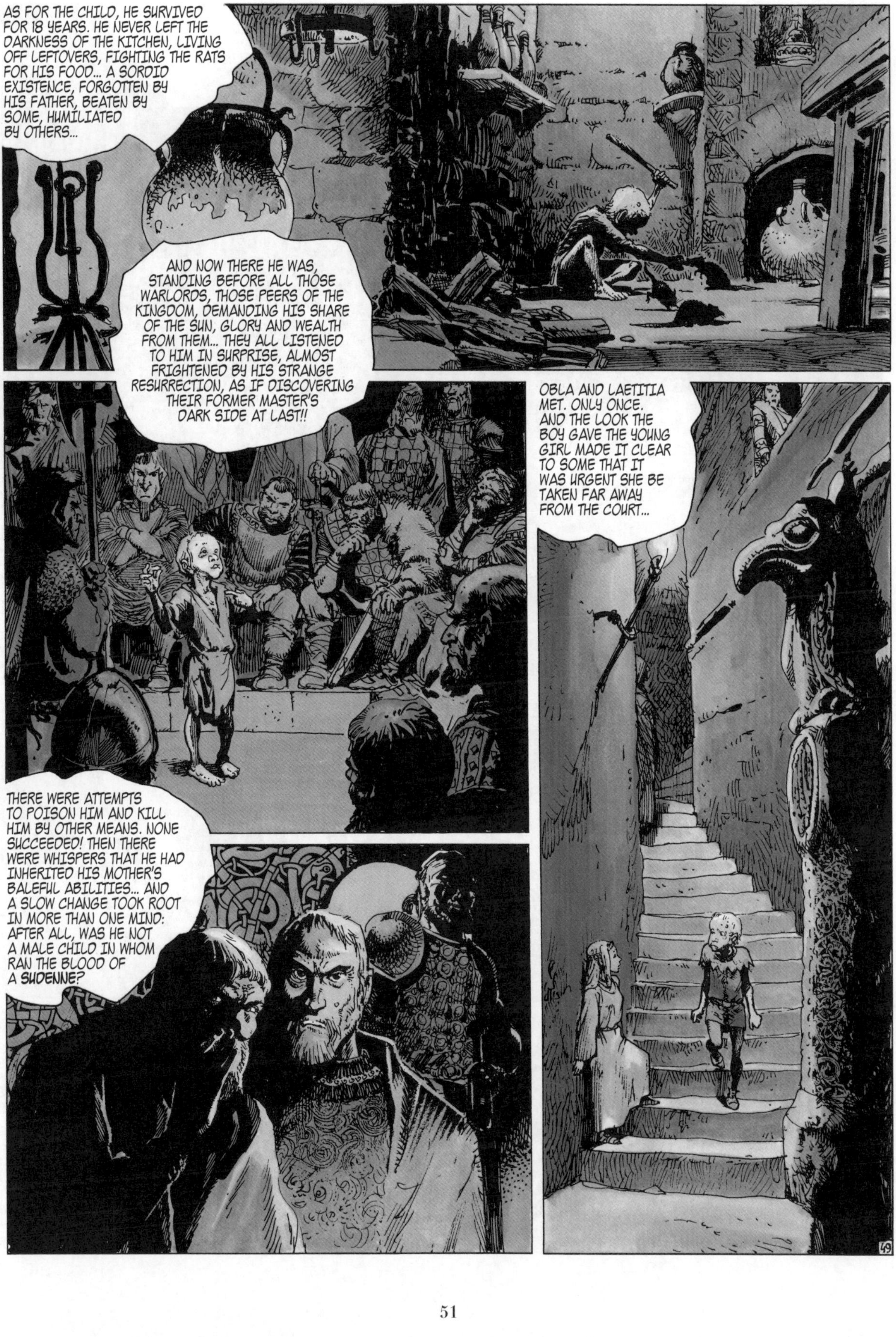
AS FOR THE CHILD, HE SURVIVED FOR 18 YEARS. HE NEVER LEFT THE DARKNESS OF THE KITCHEN, LIVING OFF LEFTOVERS, FIGHTING THE RATS FOR HIS FOOD... A SORDID EXISTENCE, FORGOTTEN BY HIS FATHER, BEATEN BY SOME, HUMILIATED BY OTHERS...
AND NOW THERE HE WAS, STANDING BEFORE ALL THOSE WARLORDS, THOSE PEERS OF THE KINGDOM, DEMANDING HIS SHARE OF THE SUN, GLORY AND WEALTH FROM THEM... THEY ALL LISTENED TO HIM IN SURPRISE, ALMOST FRIGHTENED BY HIS STRANGE RESURRECTION, AS IF DISCOVERING THEIR FORMER MASTER'S DARK SIDE AT LAST!!
THERE WERE ATTEMPTS TO POISON HIM AND KILL HIM BY OTHER MEANS. NONE SUCCEEDED! THEN THERE WERE WHISPERS THAT HE HAD INHERITED HIS MOTHER'S BALEFUL ABILITIES... AND A SLOW CHANGE TOOK ROOT IN MORE THAN ONE MIND: AFTER ALL, WAS HE NOT A MALE CHILD IN WHOM RAN THE BLOOD OF A SUDENNE?
OBLA AND LAETITIA MET. ONLY ONCE. AND THE LOOK THE BOY GAVE THE YOUNG GIRL MADE IT CLEAR TO SOME THAT IT WAS URGENT SHE BE TAKEN FAR AWAY FROM THE COURT...
49

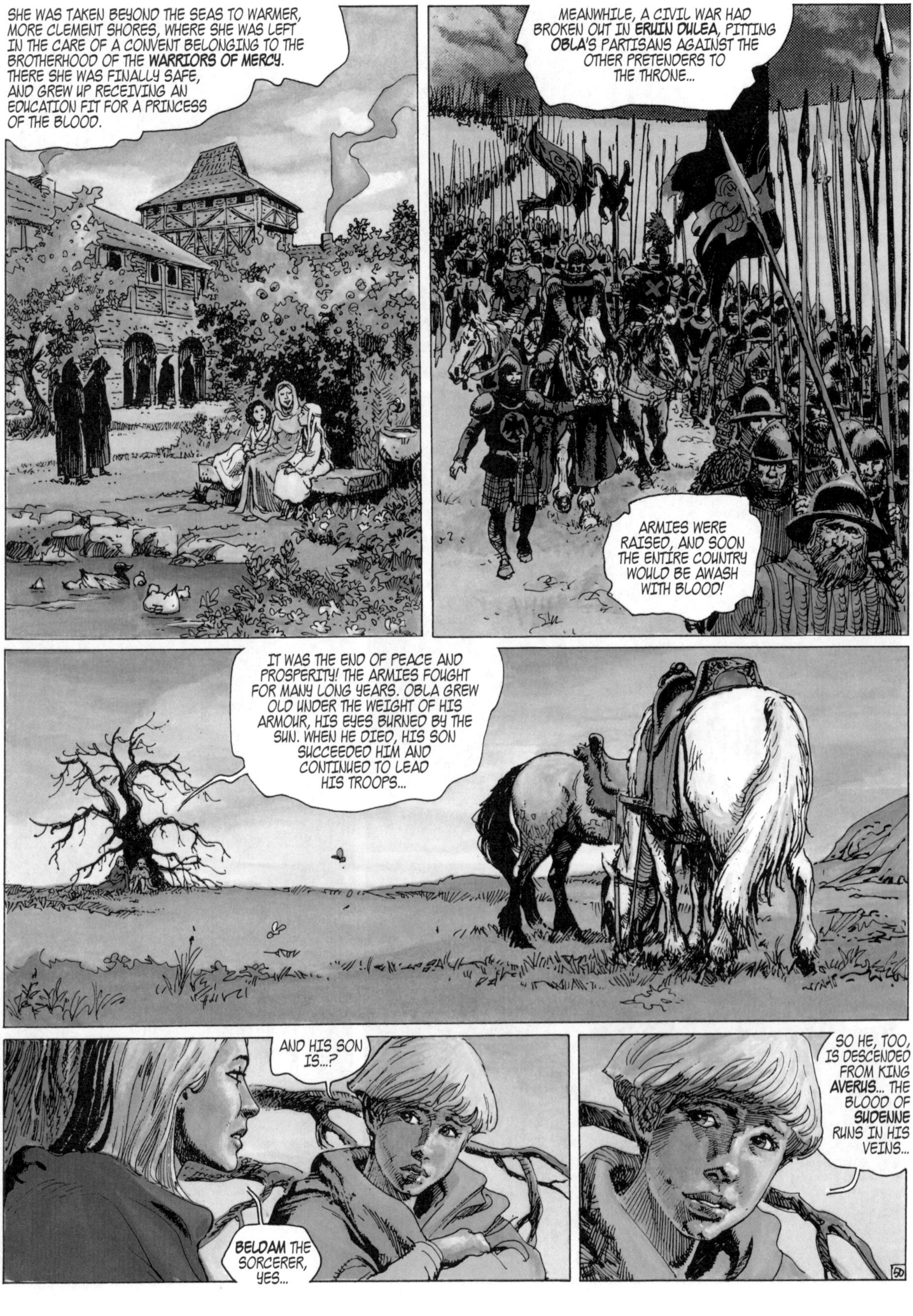

SHE WAS TAKEN BEYOND THE SEAS TO WARMER, MORE CLEMENT SHORES, WHERE SHE WAS LEFT IN THE CARE OF A CONVENT BELONGING TO THE BROTHERHOOD OF THE **WARRIORS OF MERCY**. THERE SHE WAS FINALLY SAFE, AND GREW UP RECEIVING AN EDUCATION FIT FOR A PRINCESS OF THE BLOOD.
MEANWHILE, A CIVIL WAR HAD BROKEN OUT IN **ERUIN DULEA**, PITTING **OBLA**'S PARTISANS AGAINST THE OTHER PRETENDERS TO THE THRONE...
ARMIES WERE RAISED, AND SOON THE ENTIRE COUNTRY WOULD BE AWASH WITH BLOOD!
IT WAS THE END OF PEACE AND PROSPERITY! THE ARMIES FOUGHT FOR MANY LONG YEARS. OBLA GREW OLD UNDER THE WEIGHT OF HIS ARMOUR, HIS EYES BURNED BY THE SUN. WHEN HE DIED, HIS SON SUCCEEDED HIM AND CONTINUED TO LEAD HIS TROOPS...
AND HIS SON IS...?
BELDAM THE SORCERER, YES...
SO HE, TOO, IS DESCENDED FROM KING **AVERUS**... THE BLOOD OF **SUDENNE** RUNS IN HIS VEINS...
50

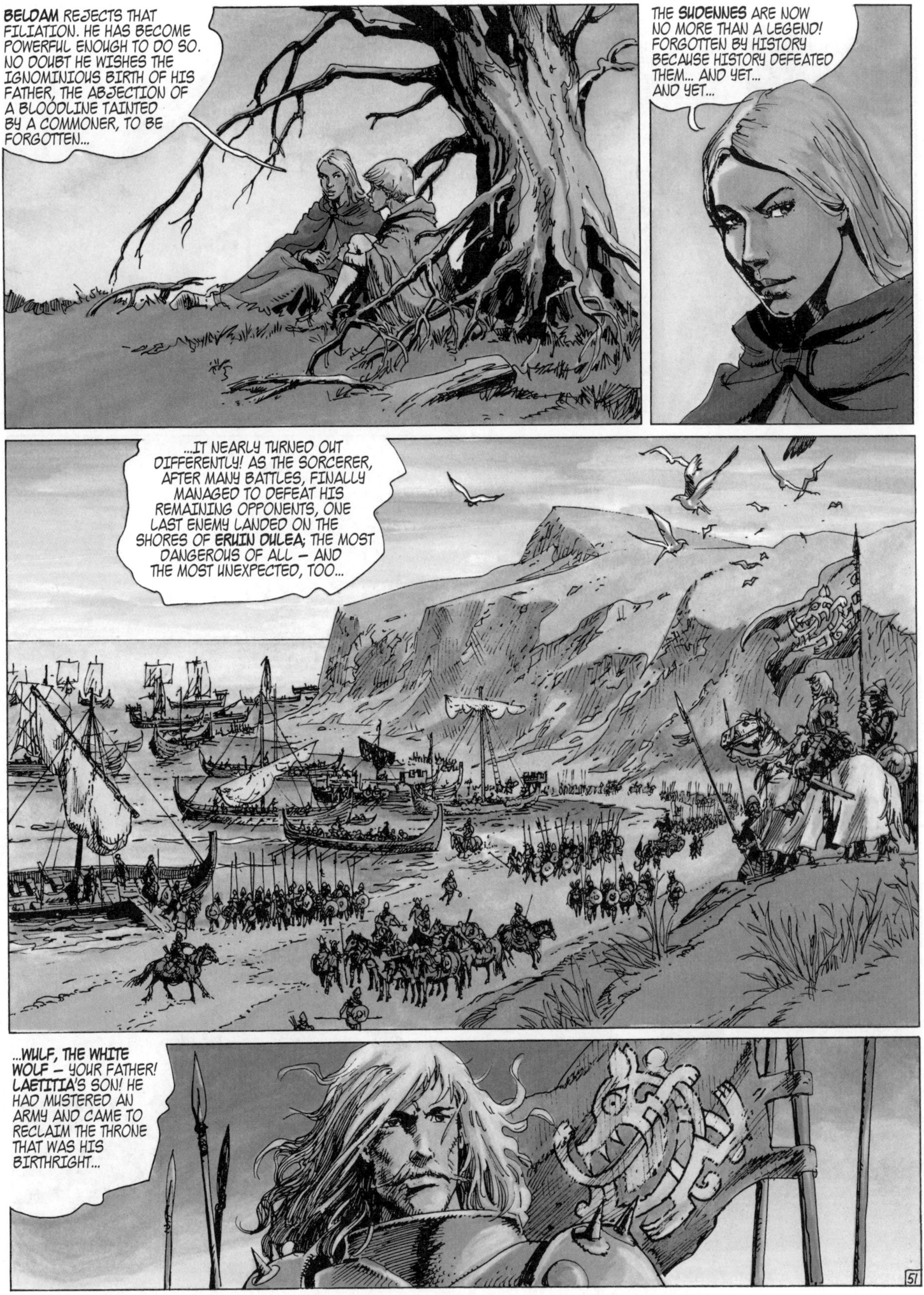
BELDAM REJECTS THAT FILIATION. HE HAS BECOME POWERFUL ENOUGH TO DO SO. NO DOUBT HE WISHES THE IGNOMINIOUS BIRTH OF HIS FATHER, THE ABJECTION OF A BLOODLINE TAINTED BY A COMMONER, TO BE FORGOTTEN...
THE SUDENNES ARE NOW NO MORE THAN A LEGEND! FORGOTTEN BY HISTORY BECAUSE HISTORY DEFEATED THEM... AND YET... AND YET...
...IT NEARLY TURNED OUT DIFFERENTLY! AS THE SORCERER, AFTER MANY BATTLES, FINALLY MANAGED TO DEFEAT HIS REMAINING OPPONENTS, ONE LAST ENEMY LANDED ON THE SHORES OF ERUIN DULEA; THE MOST DANGEROUS OF ALL – AND THE MOST UNEXPECTED, TOO...
...WULF, THE WHITE WOLF – YOUR FATHER! LAETITIA'S SON! HE HAD MUSTERED AN ARMY AND CAME TO RECLAIM THE THRONE THAT WAS HIS BIRTHRIGHT...
51

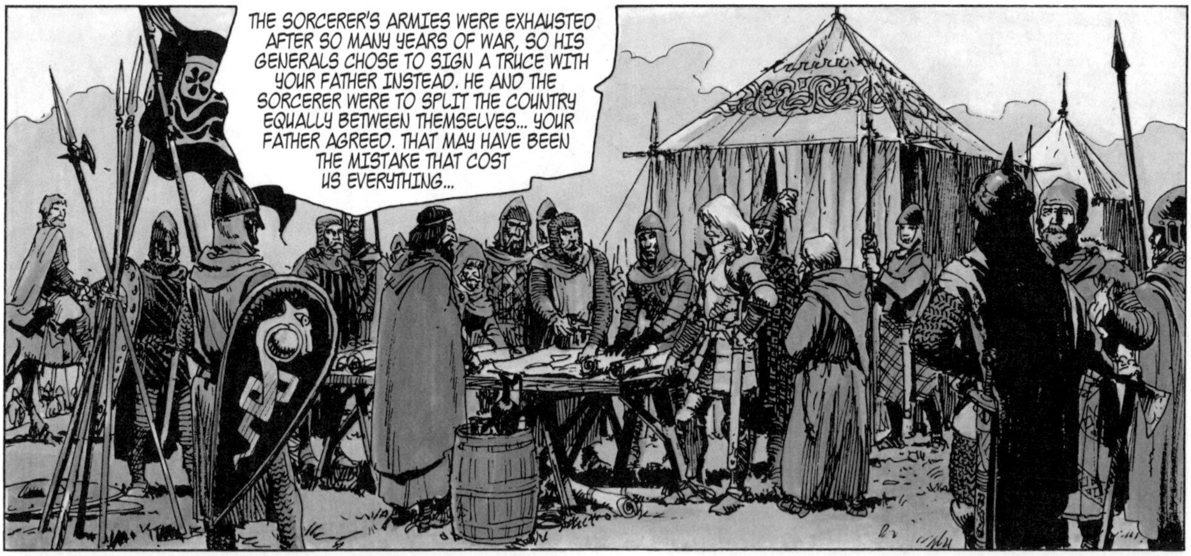
THE SORCERER'S ARMIES WERE EXHAUSTED AFTER SO MANY YEARS OF WAR, SO HIS GENERALS CHOSE TO SIGN A TRUCE WITH YOUR FATHER INSTEAD. HE AND THE SORCERER WERE TO SPLIT THE COUNTRY EQUALLY BETWEEN THEMSELVES... YOUR FATHER AGREED. THAT MAY HAVE BEEN THE MISTAKE THAT COST US EVERYTHING...

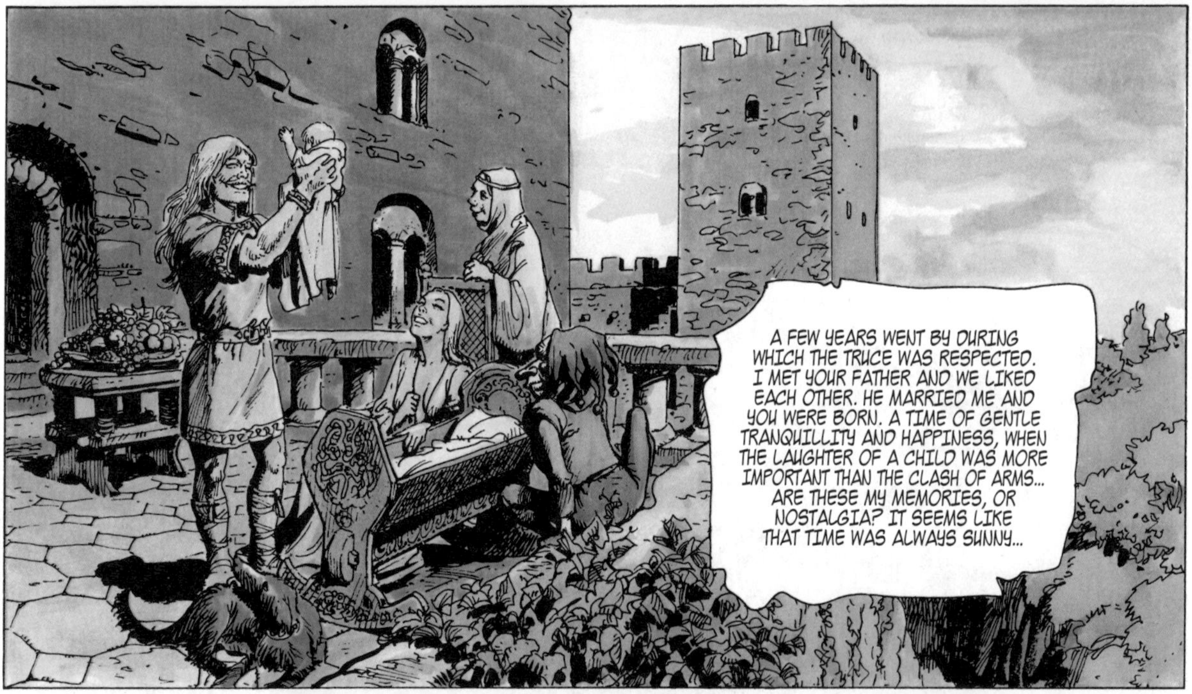
A FEW YEARS WENT BY DURING WHICH THE TRUCE WAS RESPECTED. I MET YOUR FATHER AND WE LIKED EACH OTHER. HE MARRIED ME AND YOU WERE BORN. A TIME OF GENTLE TRANQUILLITY AND HAPPINESS, WHEN THE LAUGHTER OF A CHILD WAS MORE IMPORTANT THAN THE CLASH OF ARMS... ARE THESE MY MEMORIES, OR NOSTALGIA? IT SEEMS LIKE THAT TIME WAS ALWAYS SUNNY...

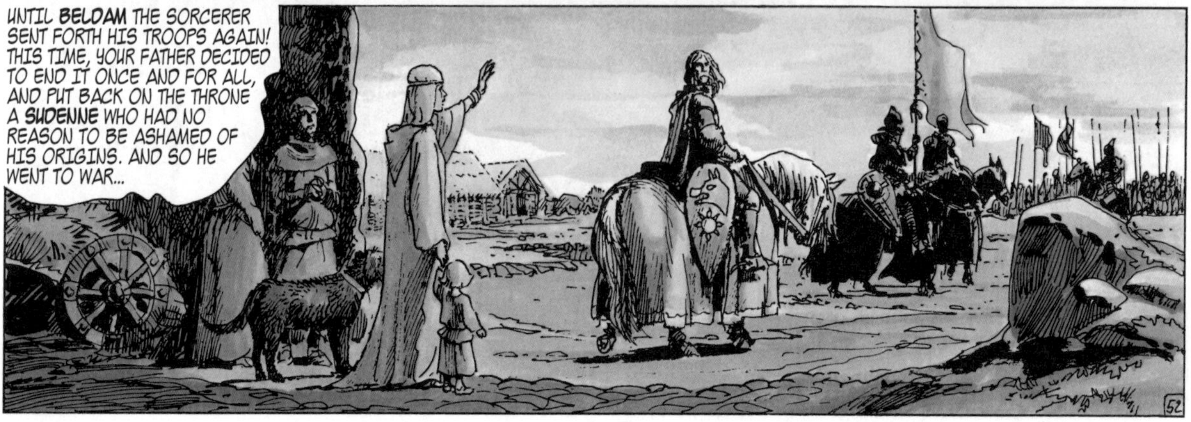
UNTIL **BELDAM** THE SORCERER SENT FORTH HIS TROOPS AGAIN! THIS TIME, YOUR FATHER DECIDED TO END IT ONCE AND FOR ALL, AND PUT BACK ON THE THRONE A **SUDENNE** WHO HAD NO REASON TO BE ASHAMED OF HIS ORIGINS. AND SO HE WENT TO WAR...
52

AND IT WAS THE GREAT BATTLE OF NYR LYNCH! A DECISIVE BATTLE, BEARER OF ALL HOPES AND ALL CURSES...

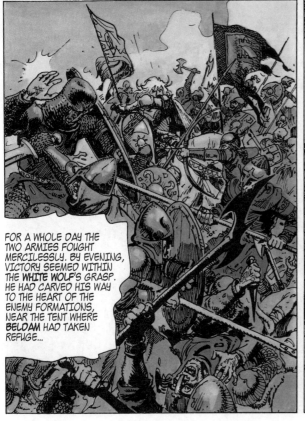

FOR A WHOLE DAY THE TWO ARMIES FOUGHT MERCILESSLY. BY EVENING, VICTORY SEEMED WITHIN THE **WHITE WOLF'S** GRASP. HE HAD CARVED HIS WAY TO THE HEART OF THE ENEMY FORMATIONS, NEAR THE TENT WHERE **BELDAM** HAD TAKEN REFUGE...

THAT WAS WHEN A THICK, BLACK CLOUD OF PESTILENTIAL VAPOURS BOILED UP OUT OF THAT TENT!

53

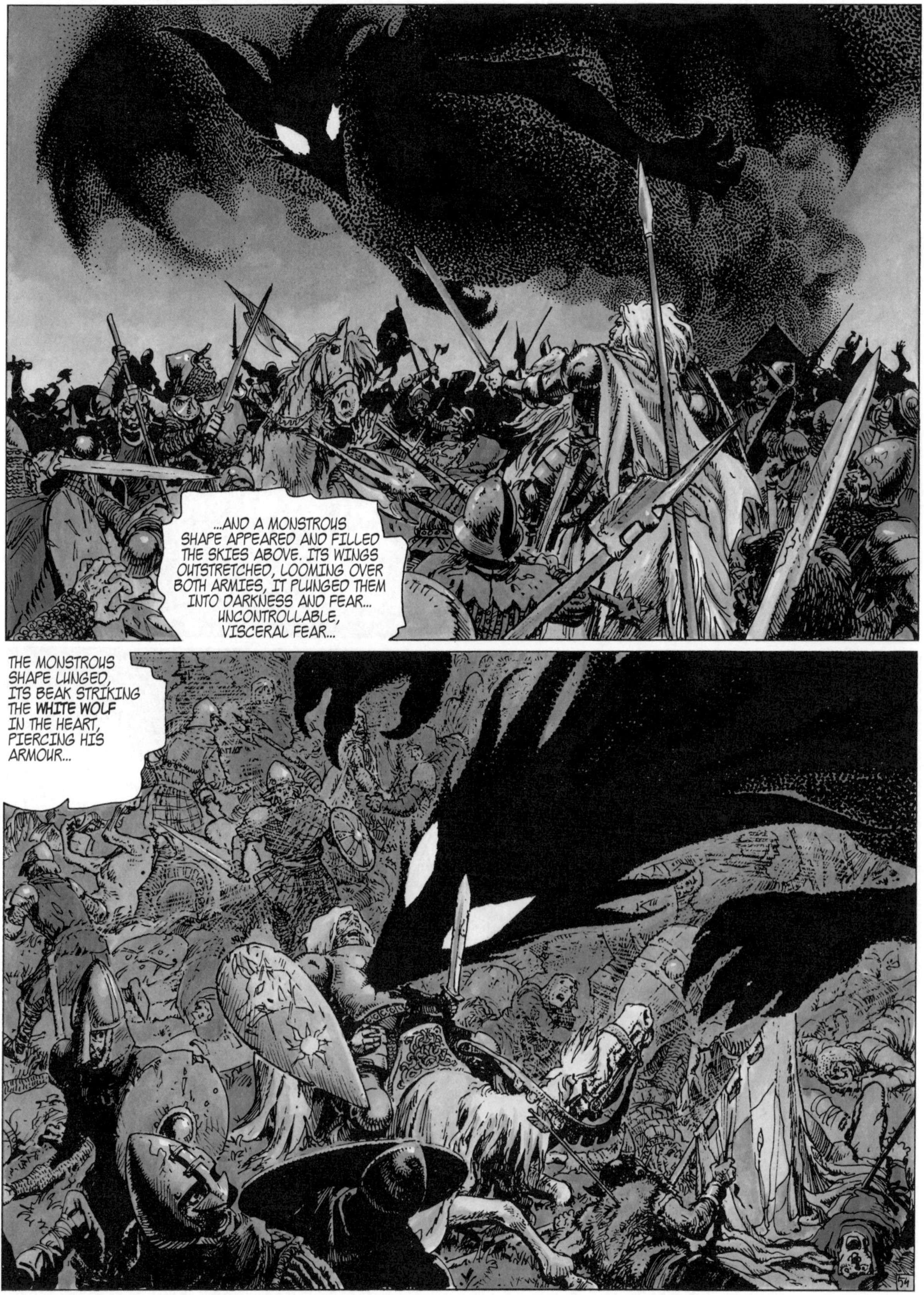
...AND A MONSTROUS SHAPE APPEARED AND FILLED THE SKIES ABOVE. ITS WINGS OUTSTRETCHED, LOOMING OVER BOTH ARMIES, IT PLUNGED THEM INTO DARKNESS AND FEAR... UNCONTROLLABLE, VISCERAL FEAR...
THE MONSTROUS SHAPE LUNGED, ITS BEAK STRIKING THE **WHITE WOLF** IN THE HEART, PIERCING HIS ARMOUR...

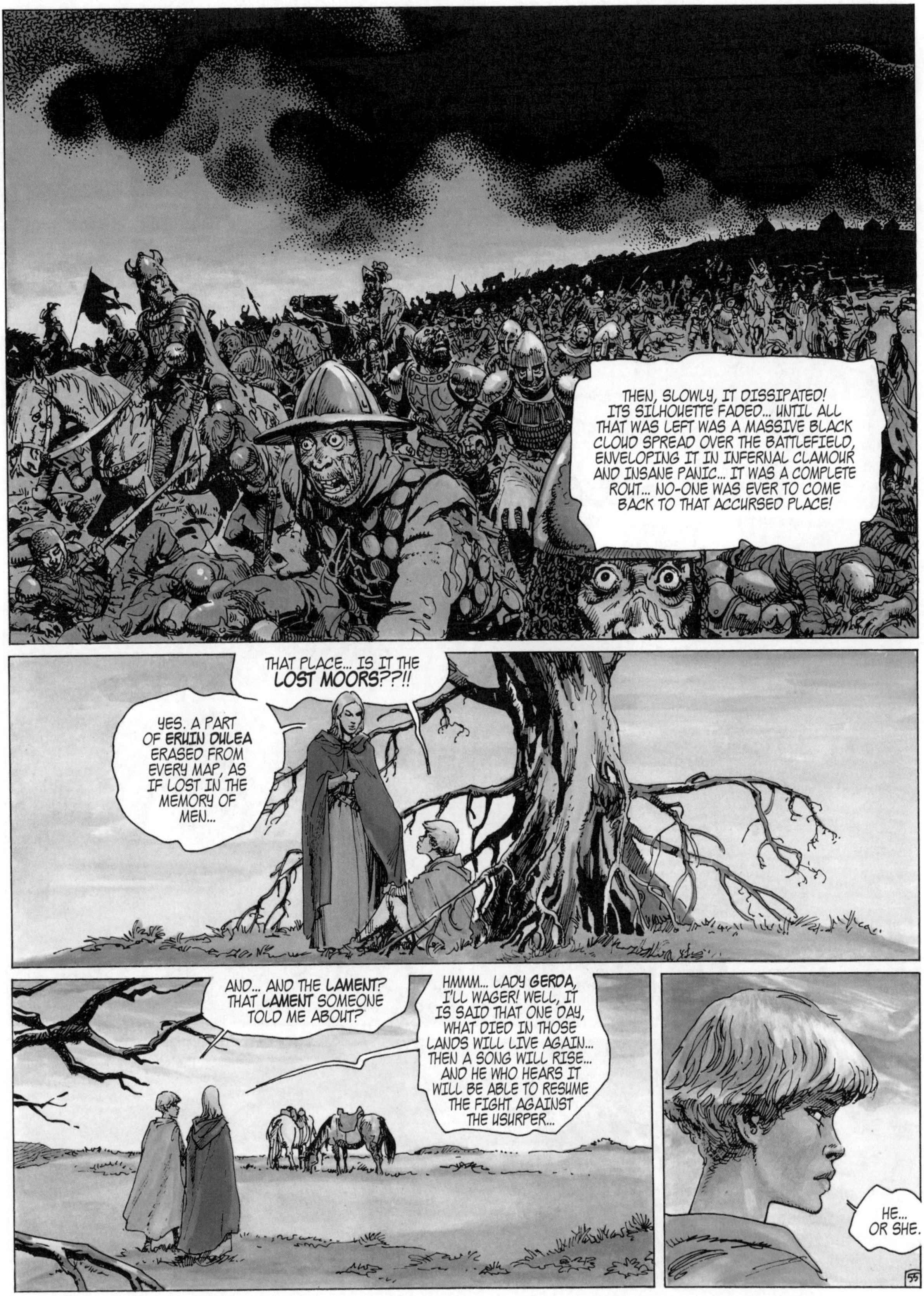
THEN, SLOWLY, IT DISSIPATED! ITS SILHOUETTE FADED... UNTIL ALL THAT WAS LEFT WAS A MASSIVE BLACK CLOUD SPREAD OVER THE BATTLEFIELD, ENVELOPING IT IN INFERNAL CLAMOUR AND INSANE PANIC... IT WAS A COMPLETE ROUT... NO-ONE WAS EVER TO COME BACK TO THAT ACCURSED PLACE!
THAT PLACE... IS IT THE LOST MOORS??!!
YES. A PART OF ERUIN DULEA ERASED FROM EVERY MAP, AS IF LOST IN THE MEMORY OF MEN...
AND... AND THE LAMENT? THAT LAMENT SOMEONE TOLD ME ABOUT?
HMMM... LADY GERDA, I'LL WAGER! WELL, IT IS SAID THAT ONE DAY, WHAT DIED IN THOSE LANDS WILL LIVE AGAIN... THEN A SONG WILL RISE... AND HE WHO HEARS IT WILL BE ABLE TO RESUME THE FIGHT AGAINST THE USURPER...
HE... OR SHE.

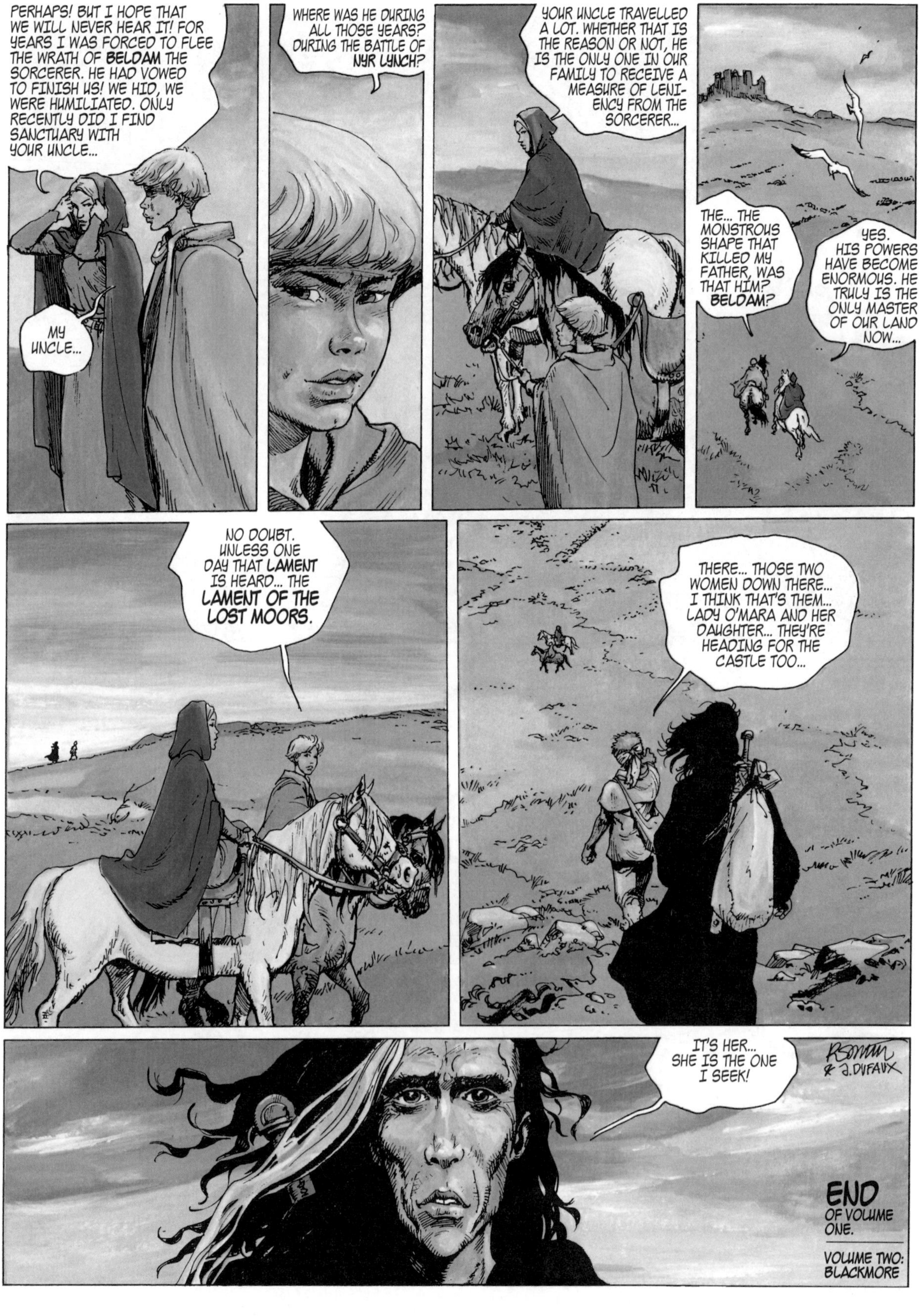
PERHAPS! BUT I HOPE THAT WE WILL NEVER HEAR IT! FOR YEARS I WAS FORCED TO FLEE THE WRATH OF BELDAM THE SORCERER. HE HAD VOWED TO FINISH US! WE HID, WE WERE HUMILIATED. ONLY RECENTLY DID I FIND SANCTUARY WITH YOUR UNCLE...
MY UNCLE...
WHERE WAS HE DURING ALL THOSE YEARS? DURING THE BATTLE OF NYR LYNCH?
YOUR UNCLE TRAVELLED A LOT. WHETHER THAT IS THE REASON OR NOT, HE IS THE ONLY ONE IN OUR FAMILY TO RECEIVE A MEASURE OF LENI-ENCY FROM THE SORCERER...
THE... THE MONSTROUS SHAPE THAT KILLED MY FATHER, WAS THAT HIM? BELDAM?
YES. HIS POWERS HAVE BECOME ENORMOUS. HE TRULY IS THE ONLY MASTER OF OUR LAND NOW...
NO DOUBT. UNLESS ONE DAY THAT LAMENT IS HEARD... THE LAMENT OF THE LOST MOORS.
THERE... THOSE TWO WOMEN DOWN THERE... I THINK THAT'S THEM... LADY O'MARA AND HER DAUGHTER... THEY'RE HEADING FOR THE CASTLE TOO...
IT'S HER... SHE IS THE ONE I SEEK!
R.SORIANO & J. DUFAUX
END OF VOLUME ONE.
VOLUME TWO: BLACKMORE

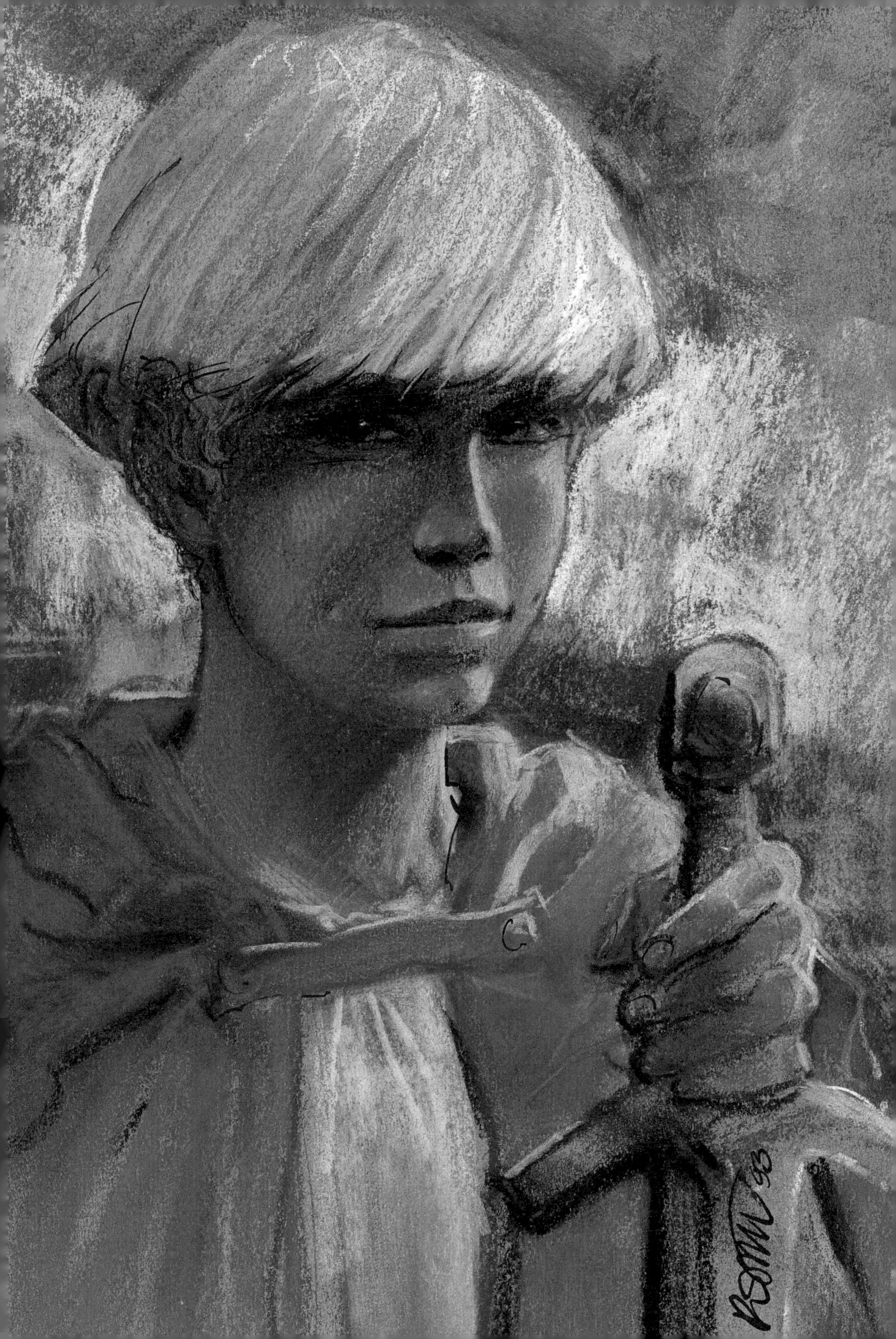

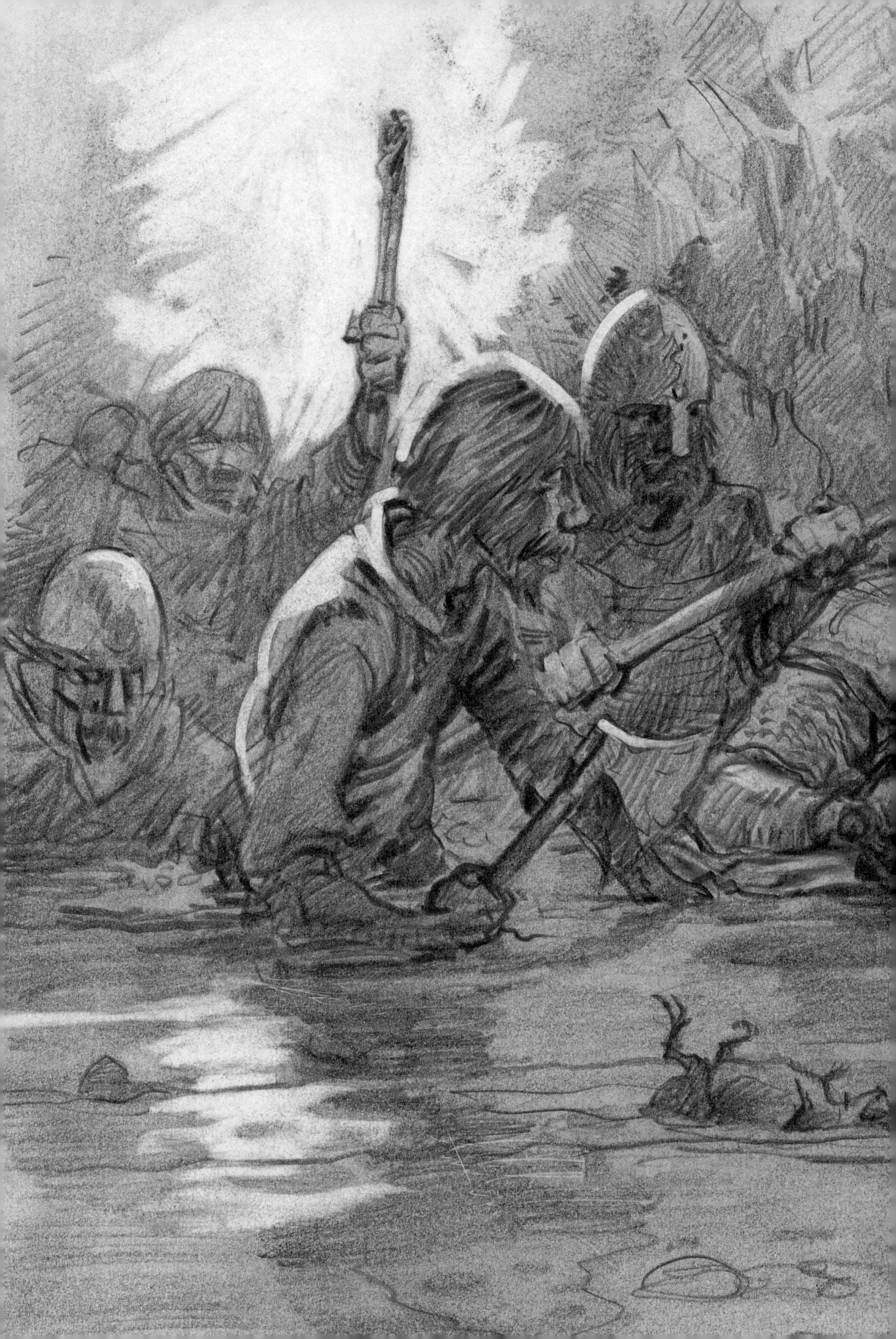

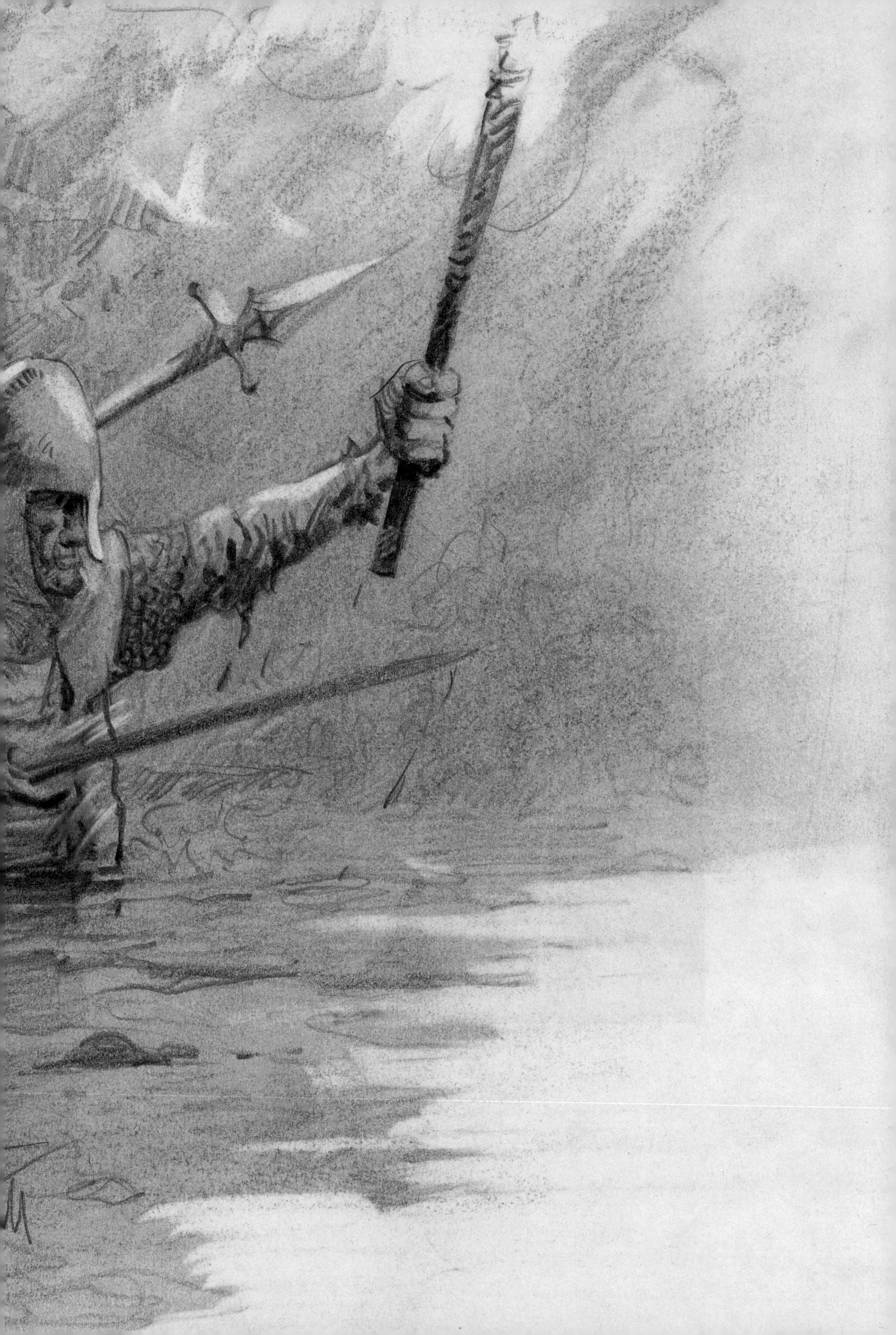

Coming soon

LAMENT OF THE LOST MOORS 2

Blackmore

ROSINSKI
DUFAUX

February 2014

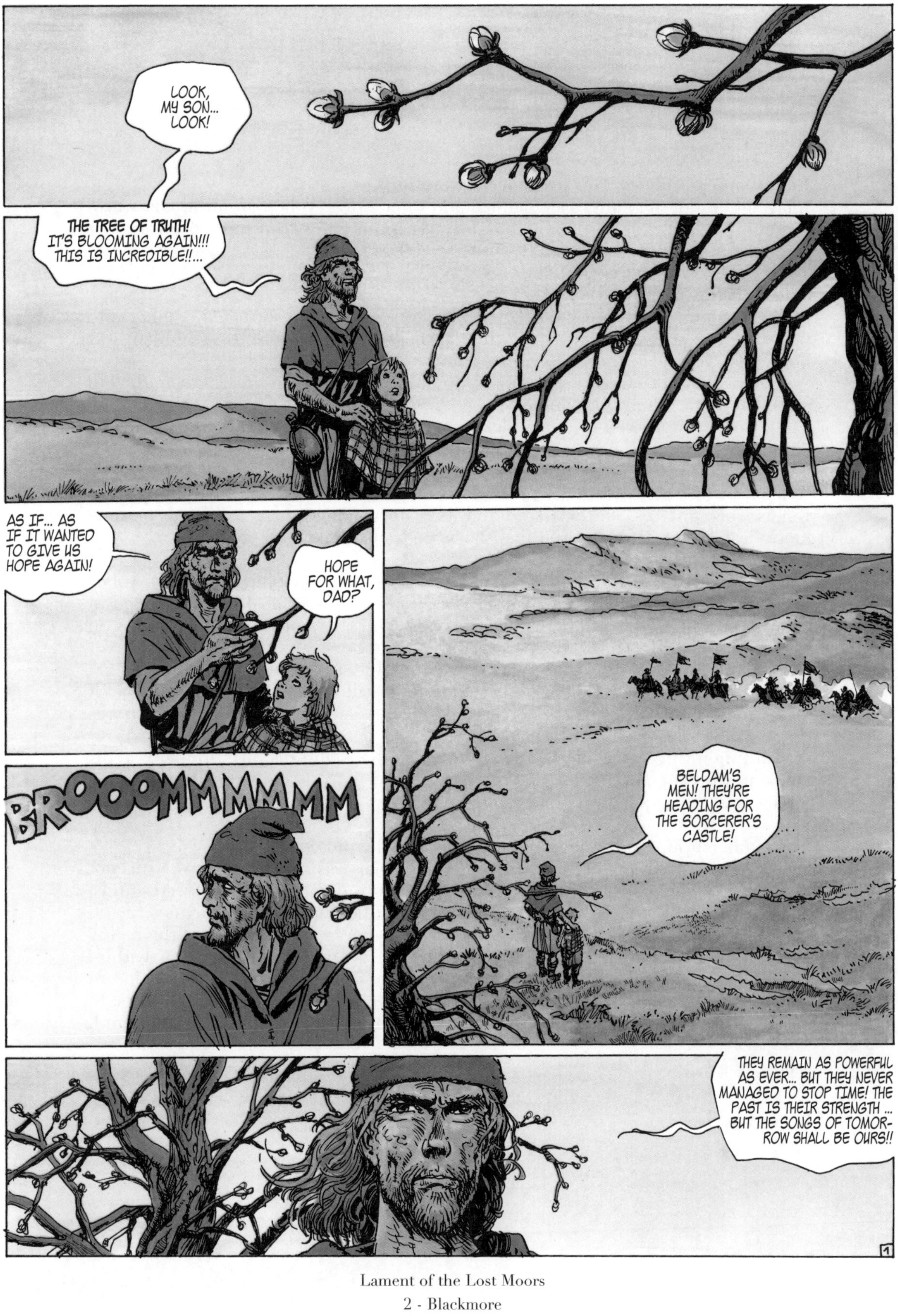
LOOK, MY SON... LOOK!
THE TREE OF TRUTH! IT'S BLOOMING AGAIN!!! THIS IS INCREDIBLE!!...
AS IF... AS IF IT WANTED TO GIVE US HOPE AGAIN!
HOPE FOR WHAT, DAD?
BROOOOMMMMMM
BELDAM'S MEN! THEY'RE HEADING FOR THE SORCERER'S CASTLE!
THEY REMAIN AS POWERFUL AS EVER... BUT THEY NEVER MANAGED TO STOP TIME! THE PAST IS THEIR STRENGTH ... BUT THE SONGS OF TOMOR-ROW SHALL BE OURS!!
1

Let us sweep aside certain preconceived notions.
Imagination doesn't suffer calculations and forecasting. When an imaginary world presents itself, it is as a self-evident truth; it cannot fall within some profit line or commercial venture.

And so it was with the Lament.
In the beginning, the idea was to tell the story of a young princess coming into power, of her struggle to dissipate the darkness of the past. And so Siobhán was born. A cycle which, from two, grew to four volumes.
A cycle proposed to Grzegorz Rosinski, an old friend, an ogre straight from the old tales, a fine travelling companion.
The manuscript arrived on his table in the most anonymous manner, without the author's name. Just the text; everything inside the text.

A small bit of an island. A few indications, landmarks on a map ravaged by time. But as work progressed, the island and its history, pulled out of oblivion, became more fleshed out, and imposed their laws, their customs, their language.

Many documents were still missing. The great fire that consumed Hascourt Abbey in 1034 saw the complete destruction of all manuscripts from the Brotherhood of the Warriors of Mercy. Those manuscripts had held a large part of the accounts on the origins of Eruin Dulea, the island of the lost moors.
That island was feared by the navigators of the time. In truth, its legend protected it, being of the kind that could scare the hardiest sailor. The stories that came of it all testified to the grave dangers that would face those who landed on those shores devoted to evil.
In truth, no prince ever had the desire to make the island his own, to increase his lands and his income by a conquest that seemed more like a squandering of his forces than the acquisition of additional ones.

Many superstitions still reigned in the courts of the old continent.
The notion of Christianity, the idea of a God that was one, not destructive, not vindictive... A new idea that only slowly made its way into often confused minds, made fearful by the many curses that befell them: famines, wars, epidemics...
And besides, everyone, from the copyist to the prince, was convinced of the reality of the power that witches had acquired on the island. Evil came from within, it could hide behind a smooth, pure appearance. Corruption of the blood led to corruption of the land, of the clans. The Lament tells us of the fight led by some to shake off the yoke of that curse, that dark web that witches had cast over the island.

Jean Dufaux